the diary of the scarlet woman

Vol. I

the diary of the scarlet woman

Vol. I

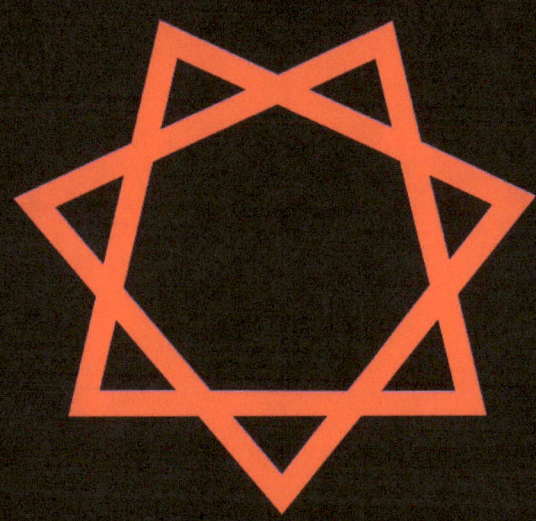

Trinity Sarah Craig

First published in 2017 by Trinity Artistix Corporation
Victoria, British Columbia
www.trixxcorp.com

♦♦♦ Copyright © 2017 Trinity Sarah Craig

All images, symbols and book formatting created by Trinity Sarah Craig
All costumes, make-up, set design by Trinity Sarah Craig
All images © Trinity Sarah Craig
Photos of The Scarlet Woman by Photon

♦♦♦ All rights reserved. No part of this publication may be reproduced or transmitted in any form or by any means, electronic or mechanical, including photocopying, recording, or by any information storage and retrieval system, without permission in writing from Trinity Artistix Corporation. Reviewers may quote brief passages.

♦♦♦ The author and publisher shall have no liability or responsibility to any person or entity regarding any loss or damage incurred, or alleged to have incurred, directly or indirectly, by the information contained in this book.

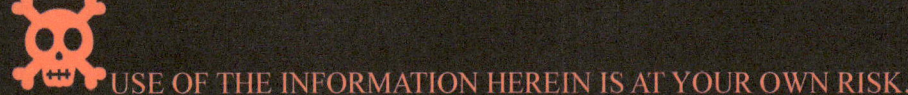USE OF THE INFORMATION HEREIN IS AT YOUR OWN RISK.

Library and Archives Canada Cataloguing in Publication

Craig, Trinity Sarah, 1974-, author
The diary of the scarlet woman / Trinity Sarah Craig.

Includes bibliographical references.
Contents: vol. 1. The diary of the scarlet woman
Issued in print format.
ISBN 978-0-9940018-6-3 (v. 1 : pbk.).

1. Spirituality. I. Title.

BL664.C33 2013
204 555-3 C2013-908166-1

••• i am •••
••• for her •••
••• wake up! •••
••• love is the law •••

Who is The Scarlet Woman? This question has been asked and answered in copious ways. Born from a vision of terror? Or is her source much more ancient and profound? A flaming presence and mysteriousness proceed her; and many throughout the Aeons have pondered her tantalizing archaic nature.

What is The Scarlet Woman? With titles like "Mother of Abominations" and "Sacred Whore" attached to her, she is an enigma to most. Aleister Crowley, the famous British magickian, professed to know her well in many of his writings. With her crimson aura bleeding through his beautiful words, he took us deeper into her mysteries. He held a lantern up in the unexplored darkness, in an effort to share his understanding of her with us.

But, as The Scarlet Woman is the representation of the Goddess, he could only travel so far down those hallowed female pathways. For the mysteries of blood eluded him, as they do with all men. This is the beauty of The Scarlet Woman. Above all, she is the most powerful priestess on the planet Earth at any given time, an office filled only when the need arises. And that time is now…

♦♦♦ introduction ♦♦♦

The Diary of The Scarlet Woman is a collection of the art and musings of the representative of the Dark Goddess on planet Earth at this time, as she researches her books that she has written, and is writing now. Most of the information is her own. Her unique point of view. Her specific magickal outlook, not available anywhere else. Some of the information is from others who also travel down the roads of magickal exploration.

The information is presented in an effort to encourage the reader to widen their own search into the magickal arts. Like magick itself, the ideas herein can be dangerous. Like The Scarlet Woman herself, it can be extreme. It can push boundaries and make you contemplate your very existence. It is gentle like the moon and ferocious like a thunder storm: sharp, with the occasional crack of lightning. If you are able to hold your head at the right angle, you will see the rainbow that suffuses the work.

You may love it and weep at the beauty of it. You may not agree. And you may not like it. But the intention behind it is true, like the feather of Ma'at. So come on this journey with The Scarlet Woman as she travels through a year of her life. Captured, like the grains in an hourglass, for your pleasure. All are welcome to have a glimpse into her private mindscape, as she shares her deep longings on the page with you. Her tricky innocence and her inherent strength laid bare.

♦♦♦ greetings ♦♦♦

My name is Trinity Sarah Craig and I am The Scarlet Woman. On March 20th 2004, I met the Dark Goddess, as retold here in these pages. It was not until afterwards that I realized the significance of that date: 100 years the anniversary of the God Horus appearing to Aleister Crowley, to tell him of his participation in the birth of the new Aeon, making him my prophet.

And so my journey as The Scarlet Woman began. The Dark Goddess told me 4 things on that spring equinox evening:

1. You are alone.
2. You are a creator of realities.
3. Everything you know is true.
4. You are the representation of the Dark Goddess on planet Earth at this time.

She activated my memory that night, and my initiation from girlhood to womanhood was begun. And now I wish to share what I know with you. As the bearer of the Holy Grail, I will tell you true: I have seen magick happen with my own eyes, many times over. It is real, true and alive. It is calling to you now; gently beckoning you to pick up the Quest for the Holy Grail…

the night i met the Dark Goddess · march 20th 2004

    i was sitting on a rock, alone at the waters edge one spring equinox night. i felt a presence standing behind me on the left. tall, cold and black. i felt that it had always been there my whole life.

    before me on the water, where the water met the opposite shore, an upside-down cross appeared on the horizon. it glowed. it was hanging above something. slowly i could make out the nests of the Fallen Angels.

    i remember my body changing. it started hunching and shrinking. growing big and strong, but not human. a voice from the presence behind me and through me, said to the image glowing on the horizon:

    "i know who you are. i know what you do. i am coming to get you. your time on Earth is short lived. you will no longer hide in the shadows. for i know who you are. i am coming to get you."

    the voice was very low and grumbly, yet penetrating. i felt it roll from me, out and around the whole world. then back to me. it came from the ground and all around me. as well as from my mouth.

    the upside down cross had become a lighthouse. a tall searching light. it started to pan across the world. it came to cover me. i had melted, dissipated and disappeared into the Earth beneath me. i was oil being sucked into the ground. the light swept harmlessly over me.

    i reformed above the ground. black oil gurgled up from the ground. it formed in front of me into a shape of myself. it became me. it sat in front of me so i could talk to myself. i was not able to look upon her behind me. hence the shiny image in front of me.

    it was like black liquid oil. it was like looking in a mirror. the mirror started talking to me. the voice was more human now. the mirror told me about myself. the mirror told me i was alone. i was told i was a creator of realities. i was told that everything i knew was true. it told me that i was the representation of the Dark Goddess on planet Earth at this time.

    the mirror talked to me a lot. i realized the dark presence was behind me again. i grabbed the back of my neck and asked harshly, "what is there?" ah, the pain. "where?" i demanded to know.

    a cold hand was laid on my shoulder, opening my back door. through the backdoor of my head, my neck. i whooshed through a tunnel. up, up, up. the coldness of space. through the blackness of the endless night. her home beyond the stars: the Void.

    i was inside. cold, black, elegant liquid webs. the belly of a great spider. a black widow. the smell was of death. putrid, heavy, old death. so overwhelming, my insides turned out. my lungs heaving.

    she, the Dark Goddess, the SpiderQueen was inside. sitting on a throne. but we were also inside of her.

    the throne was large. it had stairs. black liquid that changed when you tried to look at it. ever flowing webs that were solid and molded beautifully. an evolution of any known art movement.

    cold, intense, anger beyond anger. an intimately knowing vastness. icky, creepy, silent and huge. deeply penetrating. lonely. busy in many layers.

    near invisible cobwebs that extended and hung everywhere. webs of patterns of thought. pain in layers of time. ancient magick. beyond good or wrong. intensely devoted. dark, ancient power. from beyond time.

    i communicated with the Dark Goddess, the Guardian of the Void. i was on my knees, on the floor, in front of her. it took everything i had to be in her presence. she shared what she knows with me.

    i looked out the window. i could see the Earth far below me. hanging there in space. i saw the spider web descending all the way to it.

    suddenly, i was stuck in a cocoon in that web. cocoons like stars. somewhere before me the Earth. somewhere behind me her spidership. i saw all around me others stuck in cocoons like mine. right beside me, my brother. i could see his long black hair.

    i was stuck in my cocoon of frustration and anger. not a pretty smell. magick that has been repressed and suppressed, made to creep and crawl on its belly in order to survive. very powerful ones who have been endlessly raped, tortured and hunted.

    i was freed by my brother watcher. he appeared in glowing armour with a shining sword. he hacked and chopped through the infectious web to get to me.

climbing up to me, he cut through my cocoon. pulling my ragged corpse-like body out, he threw me over his shoulder. we started the long hike back down to Earth.

    this is when i was present once again in my body. back on the shore of the water. i stood up to walk back. i was incredibly cold and shaky. it was very dark. i was very alone.

i heard a clank, clank. i knew i was not alone at all. i felt shivers of fear. before me lining the path were Demons of every size and shape. they were the minions of the Dark Goddess. they were my minions.

Demons are angry Faeries. here to teach humans about their energetic blockages, while upon their soul journey. i was scared shitless at seeing so many Demons. i had to concentrate very tightly on walking forth and not peeing my pants. i held my head up and walked.

i knew if I let my armour slip, they would eat me alive. i walked toward the light at the top of the hill. back to reality.

there are no words to explain how painful it was to get my brains fucked by the Dark Goddess. it has taken me many years to understand and be able to communicate what i learned that night. she is inside of me. i am in service to her. i have been trained over countless lifetimes for this work. she will have me tell you the time has come again...

i claim dominion of Earth for humanity. i will the frequency of love free of conditions, in service to the Goddess. i command all things outside of love free of conditions in service to the Goddess to be released to the centre of the Earth. release, release, release, release: spirit, mind, body and emotions, release to the centre of the Earth.

this experience happened to me on march 20th, 2004. exactly one hundred years to the day, that the God Horus appeared to aleister crowley. to tell him he would serve as the prophet for the new aeon.

the Void is the afterlife. it is the place where souls are processed for their next round of reincarnation. you stay for just a brief visit. you experience it in many ways and on many levels. it is a source of inspiration. it is vast, ancient and unknowable.

the Void has a Guardian. she is known throughout many ages and cultures, by many names. she is the Dark Goddess, the Nameless One, the Crone and Grandmother Spider. she is giver of life and death. her time of power is the three days of the dark of the Moon when the Sun is not reflected upon its surface. she is then able to express her darkness.

think of her as Grandmother Spider weaving and knitting at the fire. she is in the Void. a shall around her shoulders. a woven rug underneath her foot. she has a huge cauldron that she presides over. it is boiling and frothing. the bubbles come up, live, and then pop, falling back down into the Cauldron of Creation. she is the cunt hole that the Metaverse impregnates. the cauldron is the womb. the bubbles are Universes.

Dark Goddess is noted in many cultures. tibet calls her the Black Dakini. india refers to her as Kali. egyptians called her as Neith, Nuit, Nu, or Nit, Goddess of weaving. american natives name her Spider Grandmother, the Creatrix of the world. the hopi call her Spider Old-Woman. Arachne by the greeks, Aunt Nancy in the west indies, Jorogumo by the japanese and the Teotihuacan: Spider Woman. in the andaman islands, she is known as Biliku. slavic cultures call her Baba Yaga. she is known as Dada by the african dogon, a great spider who weaves matter. the Celts named her the Morrighan.

the Void is the energetic gateway between our Universe and the Metaverse. the Dark Goddess is the Guardian of this gateway. she maintains what is known as the Book of Souls. she keeps track of all the comings and goings of all the souls as they work at completing their journey throughout all of their incarnations.

she is the Soul Administrator. she is the Mother that births-in this dimensional reality. she is the Mother of all the gods. she is the Creatrix of the Universe. all the gods come from her, as she is the first. and they will return through her. her darkness is the womb and the tomb...

Crone says

and the Crone says:
the time has come again...
when humans do not respect the wisdom of their elders or their wives
when they become greedy and exploitive
when they follow war-like gods
who preach violence and conquest
when they have forgotten love and caring
when they evade responsibility
they have no honour
therefore the angry Crone curses humans and their gods into destruction
using her dread maternal power to devour the gods she brought forth
her curse is irresistible. her curse echoes
and the gods themselves go mad
in the final paroxysms of the Earths rebirth...

calling magick children

i am The Scarlet Woman, Daughter of the Dark Goddess
i claim dominion of Earth for humanity
i will the frequency of love free of conditions in service to the Goddess
come home children of magick
the oasis of the new aeon is calling
the gates of Paradise are fastly closing
i sound the Call of the SpiderQueen
come children of magick
come home

i am

i am what i am. it is what is. it will be what it will be...

witch

witches?

abrahadabra

four

north   south   east   west
fire   air   earth   water
spirit   mental   physical   emotional
wand   knife   shield   cauldron

δ...o

death = orgasm

Precession

Precession of the Equinoxes - created by the wobble of the Earths axis which turns in a circle and points to each constellation in the sky (like a gyroscope). a full cycle lasting 25 290 years. the Earth entering each zodiacal age every 2 160 years. we have now entered the age of aquarius. a time where there are no masters...

magick party

theres a party and your invited! leave your judgment at the door! witches, warlocks, Faeries and more...

island time

   "…choose ye an island! fortify it! dung it about with enginery of war! i will give you a war-engine. with it ye shall smite the peoples; and none shall stand before you.
   lurk! withdraw! upon them! this is the law of the battle of conquest: thus shall my worship be about my secret house. get the stélé of revealing itself; set it in thy secret temple-and that temple is already aright disposed-& it shall be your kiblah for ever. it shall not fade, but miraculous colour shall come back to it day after day. close it in locked glass for a proof to the world.
   this shall be your only proof. i forbid argument. conquer! that is enough. i will make easy to you the abstruction from the ill-ordered house in the victorious city. thou shalt thyself convey it with worship, o prophet, though thou likest it not. thou shall have danger & trouble. ra-hoor-khu is with thee. worship me with fire & blood; worship me with swords & with spears. let the woman be girt with a sword before me: let blood flow to my name. trample down the heathen; be upon them, o warrior, i will give you of their flesh to eat!
   sacrifice cattle, little and big: after a child. but not now. ye shall see that hour, o blessed Beast, and thou the scarlet concubine of his desire!..." oh ya - i live in the city of victoria, on vancouver island…
~ aleister crowley - *book of the law*

come into my parlour

come into my parlour said the spider to the fly. i have a little something here…

quarantined

Earth was quarantined after the Fallen Angel Virus arrived...

Creatrix

Goddess + God = Creatrix

mushrooms

Faeries are real... watch out for little dudes with curly shoes. they hide in the shadows.
and around the stems of fat mushrooms...

eggs are us

you exist in 12 dimensions. the 13th (the Void) is the hand of the Dark Goddess that holds all the dimensions together like an egg. and lay in-between each dimension...

the egg

minky pants

i saw a mink at the beach today...

yuk

there are over 14 000 man made chemicals added to food...

quit it!

stressed out? quit caffeine...

when women ruled

i remember a time when women ruled just like men do now. men were near neanderthals and women were studying the stars because of their blood connection to the Moon. women invented mathematics, calendars, measurement, ritual
(~ judy grahn - *blood, bread & roses*)
we used to keep men in cages because they would always attack our villages and try to rape us. on the dark and full Moons we would have ceremonies and bring men out of their cages, tie them to altars and fuck them until they died. offerings to the Goddess...

flood

there are over 600 legends concerning the great flood

Winter Solstice

merry Winter Solstice! shortest day of the year, beginning of the new year and the return of the Sun...

Paradise singing inside you

Paradise is inside of you. you can reach the Creatrix through your heart. can you hear them singing?

harlequin

spiral

every living being grows in the same spiral. according to the fibonacci sequence (0 1 1 2 3 5 8 13 21...)
straight lines do not exist on planet Earth. they are alien constructs...

bleach

tampons are made with bleach. same for toilet paper. buy toilet paper and tampons made with hydrogen peroxide - not bleach. it is wise to think about what chemicals you are putting in contact with your sacred parts!

r over b

reincarnation aces over bloodline every time...

death

death is life. the day is killed for the night. the mouse perishes for the fox. the climax slowly dies...
killing is birthing. energy never dies - it is only ever transformed...

Babalon

"this is Babalon, the true mistress of the Beast; of Her, all his mistresses on lower planes are but avatars..."
~ aleister crowley - *the cry of the 16th aethyr, which is called lea*

stars

lighting a match in a quartz crystal cave...

oceans

the ocean is like a vagina - beautiful but sometimes smelly...

churchie

church - where you go if you want your soul eaten

Demons

when people are possessed by Demons they usually are cranky, quick to anger, have addictions, are high strung, have really obsessive behavioral patterns, are controlling, aggressive, violent, try to get others to do things for them and have shifty eyes. Demons are not allowed to actually manifest in the 3rd dimension, so they use a human host.
but their energy is harmful for the human, that is why the strange behaviour occurs...

Otherwise

evil does not exist. it is just another christian wet dream. but Otherwise certainly does…

five

quintessence...

instant manifestation

apocalypse. when humans will ascend back to the 5th and 6th dimensions. where your thoughts manifest instantly...

Nuit

"(nuit) nu-isis is Nature purged of false accretions such as ethics, morality and man-made laws..."
~ kenneth grant - *aleister crowley and the hidden god*

christ

i do not believe in the christian version of christ
why would i celebrate their made up date of his birthday?
nice example of how christians have weaseled themselves into your mind...

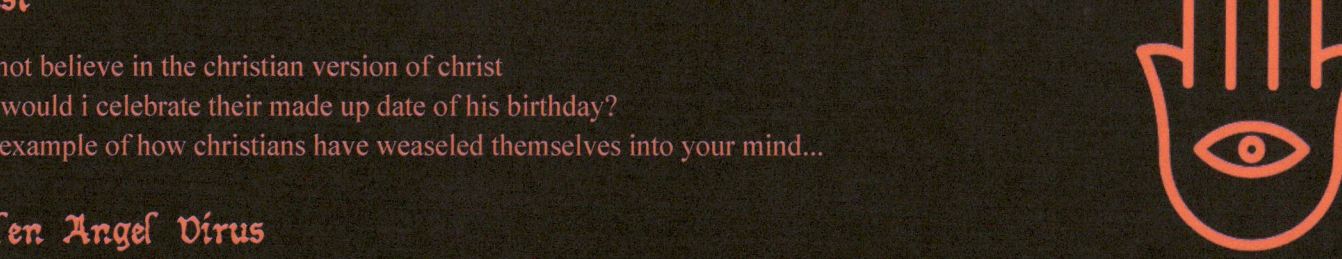

fallen Angel Virus

the war in heaven started roughly 250 billion years ago with the creation of what is know as the Fallen Angel Virus…

venus

the elliptical path of venus (when she travels around the Sun every eight years) forms a perfect pentagram
she is the only celestial body that creates a flawless geometric figure in its orbit in the Universe…

lost souls

christians tell me i am lost soul… do they ever consider that maybe they are the ones that are lost?
its strange how we can project our emotions outwards onto complete strangers. the sacred mirror reflects our own issues right back to us. you will only ever see what you dislike about yourself in others…

satan

   "satan was never mentioned in the old testament. there were 'satans' rarely mentioned. they were portrayed as obedient servants. who performed specific functions of strategic obstruction for the gods. the hebrew root word of satan is STN which is defined as opposer, adversary or accuser. members of political opposition party would have been called satans. judges (accusers) were called satans.
   it wasnt until roman imperial times (4th century) that satan was fabricated as an opposer to God. the roman faith was based wholly of the subservience of the people to the bishops. so an enemy was needed to scare the illiterate peasants into going to church. so if you did not offer absolute obedience to the church you would have your soul taken from you by 'satan.'
   so those romans were really trying to find a way to slip 'satan' into the old testament. lo and behold there was this serpent! so one serpent + one satan = happy controlling romans. ironically god in the old testament lied to adam (dont eat from the tree or you will die). it was the snake who was honest and told adam the tree would free him. isnt it scary how people have given their power over to a book and belief from the 4th century? (archaic!). its not that the bible is wrong. it has just been so mistranslated. by a bunch of sexually repressed, homophobic, brainwashed, gynophobic, fear mongering elitist priests..."
~ laurence gardner - *genesis of the grail kings*

human calendar

the humans of Earth have always used a calendar with 13 Moons. with a month having 28 days (just like a womans blood cycle). pope gregory XIII forced the 12 month calendar onto the world… (as usual the pushy roman catholics trying to force everyone to do their bidding). the 7th century mayan prophet pacal votan said; 'if humanity wishes to save itself from biospheric destruction it must return to living in natural time'

i went to faerieland

i went to Faerieland. there are no words to describe how intense it was. like life and death happening at the same time. the most beautiful and the most horrible. it took my breath away. they sure know how to party!
you can go to… you just have to believe…

Otherwise Harlots

way to go all you Otherwise harlots! thats right your not whores. because at least whores have the sense to charge for their wares. you just give yourselves away for free! where is the mystery? where is the unveiling? wheres the romance? youre cheap! you look cheap! you smell cheap!
where are the battle Goddesses of old? oh thats right, im right here! coming to kick the weak willed women right in the twat! wake up! you are being taken advantage of! think for yourself instead of doing what you are told to do!

arent you tired of being service industry slaves? arent you tired of being second class citizens? arent you tired of being all anxious because your not good enough, or thin enough, or pretty enough? fuck this world, lets make our own...

Angelic

"this is the recipe for seeing Angels... he said as he stirred the mixture..."
~ ross haven - *the sin eater's last confessions*

psycho

the secret government is pathologically psychotic...

id like to know

when did we exchange the Laws of Nature for material values?

ads

advertising = occult symbolism in uncaring hands. imagine if those fuckers actually used their hocus pocus to support humans instead of sucking them dry of money, energy and brains...

dead

when the church missionized the world they murdered over 95% of the worlds tribal population in under four hundred years... these tribes were from all of the races including whites...

choices

you are either making a choice that evolves you or de-evolves you...

torus

a torus is like a doughnut.
the magnetic field of your heart, your body, the Earth, the Sun and all living beings spin like a torus...

Dragons are alive

Dragons are alive. they live and swim in the black oil in the ground. thats why the Fallen Angels dig up oil, looking for the Dragons. Dragons guard the entrances of crystal caves in the ground. the caves have gold, rubies, diamonds. the caves lead to Faerieland. you can go there if you want - but dont drink what the Faeries offer you. or you could stay there forever...

Otherwise

the Otherwise side put the circle around the star to imprison ignorant witches... "the pentagram was also the "place" (prison) where the first pre-cosmic offspring had to be put in order for the ordered cosmos to appear" - wikipedia

latin

so witches back in northern u.k. held off the roman invasions as long as we could. (were talking around 1st century). kinda like the last magickal stand against the church. because they had subdued everywhere else in the world...

then the romans conquered and raped all the priestesses and murdered most of the druids. cutting down all the sacred forests. to say the obvious the romans and their church are the opposite of witches. so then why are all the witches and magickians today speaking latin in their rituals? latin is a Fallen Angel language...

plastic sucks

the plastic bottle you carelessly toss on the ground can take 1 000 000 (yes that is a million) years to biodegrade...

Horned One

The Horned One, Lord of the Forest is the consort of the Goddess. he defends her honour and stands as her protector and warrior...

time & tpace

even though your body appears solid, in reality there are atoms with spaces between them. these atoms consist of a nucleus with electrons spiraling around them. if there was a microscopic creature looking at you, to him you would appear just like a solar system. spiraling bodies with huge spaces between them...

neith

neith

egyptian mother goddess
responsible for creating matter by weaving it
same as spider goddess called Dada of the dogon, Spider Grandmother by native americans, Arachne by the Greeks
Aunt Nancy in the west indies, Jorogumo by the japanese
and Spider Woman by the navajo
and Old Spider Woman by the hopi...
her headress is exactly the same image as a complicated quantum string interaction
(string theory - quantum physics)

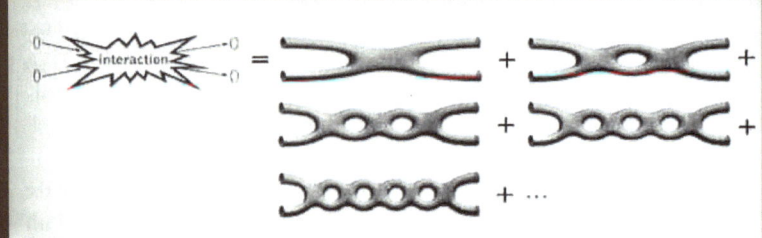

The net influence each incoming string has on the other comes from adding together the influences involving diagrams with ever more loops.

neith's catouche displays two other quantum string interactions...

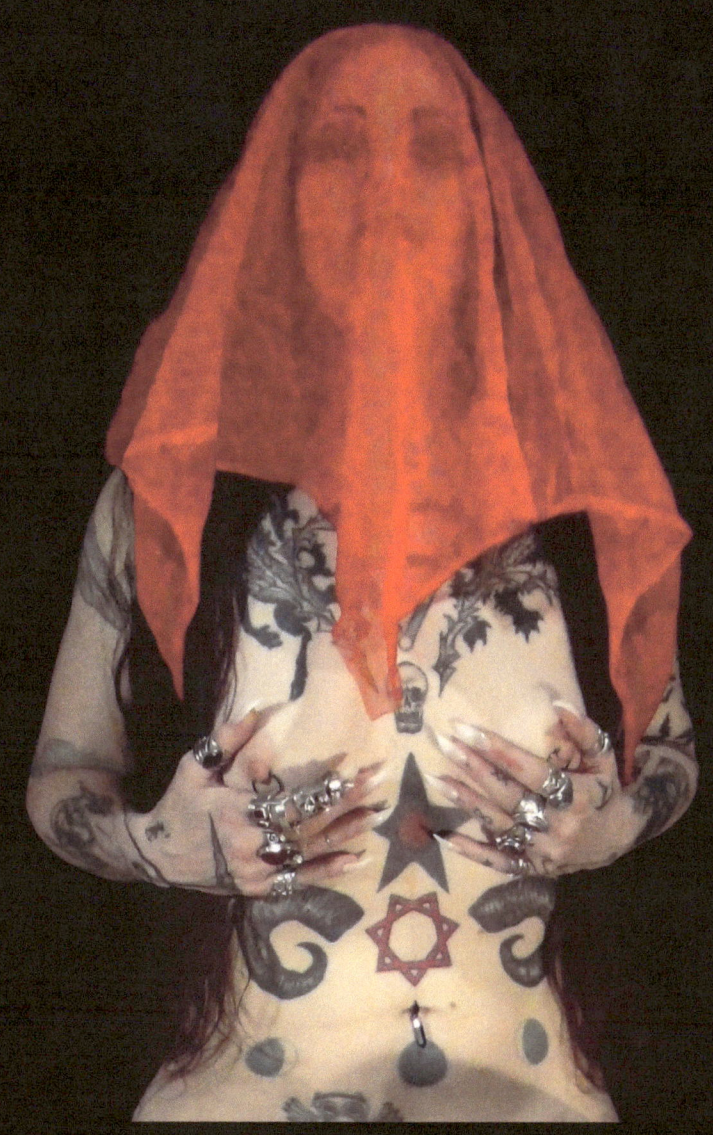

thoth

thoth = son of enki = tehuti = ruler of atlantis = hermes = raismes of aphra = *the emerald tablets of thoth* = the illuminated enochian master = mercury = zoroaster = quetzalcoatl = viracocha = builder of the pyramid = anunnaki = started the mayan calendar = *book of thoth* by aleister crowley = contributor to the book *the ancient secret of the flower of life*...

validity

the truth never needs to be proven...

received

human thoughts can be received by esoteric crystal radio receivers and relayed into a computer which can store the thoughts in terms of information bits. then these thought patterns can in turn be displayed on a computer screen and printed out on a piece of paper. these experiments were so successful they started a project called the montauk project. ya, that was back in the 1940's...

nefertiti

i remember being nefertitis daughter scota. when i saw her bust in berlin she activated my memories...

merlin

prophecy says merlin sleeps in a crystal cave. he will wake when arthur
calls him to come back at that fateful time when we need him the most!...

toxicity

why do we get off on toxicity? look at the state of the world today. it is because it is toxic and somehow
we like it or we just dont give a shit. this is the Fallen Angel Virus...

wondering

i wonder what the shift smells like...

calling all magickians

"the ancient message comes, calling the kindred to take flight and gather together. only then can they hope to survive the
cruel season to come...."
~ "Heroes" tv show

crystal graves

the graves of the Fallen Angels - using charged crystals and magickal techniques to attract, contain and harness the energy
released from the frequency net placed around the Earth...

quietly died

the old aeon has quietly died. its power structure and foundation has been changed, altered and remodeled.
the authority of the old aeon is quickly realizing its power source is gone.
some have a hard time letting go because they are and will be unable to do so.
the new aeon is blooming in the hearts and minds of the new aeon magickians. some do not even recognize themselves
as the new leaders of the world. it is time to awaken, step into your authentic self and take up the reins of control.
you are free and free from rules...

jesus pharaonic Dragon king

   "jesus was one in a long lineage of pharaonic dragon messiah kings. a druid and a magus (magickian), this lineage
descends from the sumerian god-king enki. you may know him by his other names: samuel, lucifer or ptah. jesus was
known to perform what the christians later termed the black mass. which is the consuming of virgin menstrual blood
for its high melatonin content. melatonin increases higher brain function, clairvoyance, sensitivity and intuition. the
characteristics of the leaders of old. the church has taken our true history and perverted it to its own ends and put in its
place an illusion maintained through fear..."
~ nicholas de vere – *the dragon legacy*

oracle

the oracle would sit over vapours coming from deep inside the Earth on a three legged stool...

stats

our whole society is based on statistics. the thing is statistics are not real... just because it happened to one thousand

people does not mean it will happen to me!
statistics are a false system of measurement placed upon humans. by allowing statistics to rule our lives, we are not in control of our realities. if we are not in control - then who or what is?

spiritual not physical

apocalypse is not about weapons. it is a spiritual rendering. food, water and shelter are not the issue.
whether or not you have a soul is...

fibonacci sequence

fibonacci sequence: 0.0.1.1.2.3.5.8.13.21.34.55.89.144.233... everything in nature grows according to the same spiral. every single plant, animal, human, crystal, sea shells, and the Universe. all known organic structures grow in the exact replica of this spiral. it is the spiral of life.
thats why when you think of how are world is designed with roads, telephone wires, buildings, numbers, furniture... pretty much everything we build is straight. straight lines do not occur in nature!
no wonder the world is whacked and out of balance...

straight lines do not exist on Earth...

apocalypse

apocalypse is coming! superconsciousness! your thoughts will manifest instantly. thats why the authority creates war because they really want you to buy into it and create more. fear = more fear. if our thoughts are full of ecstasy then ecstasy we will create. it is a good idea to control your thoughts (that is the study of magick). and not have them controlled by tv, music, politics, media, etc.

when you start seeing giant robots running down the street and everyone starts losing it, remember what ive said and get yourself out to the woods, free of man made structures and draw a magick circle in the dirt. sit inside of it, and call to the four directions, Goddess below and God above. you should be okay...

upsidedown pentagram

a pentagram? an upside-down pentagram? a star is a star is a star. whether you turn it upside-down or not.
if i turn you upsidedown does that make you evil?

seer

"the seers in the early days of the aeon of osiris foresaw the manifestation of this coming aeon in which we now live, and they regarded it with intense horror and fear, not understanding the precession of the aeons, and regarding every change as catastrophe. this is the real interpretation of, and the reason for, the diatribes against the Beast and The Scarlet Woman in the xiii, xvii and xviii-th chapters of the apocalypse; but on the tree of life, the path of gimel, the Moon, descending from the highest, cuts the path of teth, leo, the house of the Sun, so that the woman in the card may be regarded as a form of the Moon, very fully illuminated by the Sun, and intimately united with him in such wise as to produce, incarnate in human form, the representative or representatives of the lord of the aeon. she rides astride the Beast; in her left hand she holds the reins, representing the passion which unites them. in her right she holds aloft the cup, the Holy Grail aflame with love and death. in this cup are mingled the elements of the sacrament of the aeon."
~ aleister crowley - *book of thoth*

pain

pain and disease are caused by the energy in your body being blocked. if you can figure out the lesson the pain is trying to teach you - it will go away. usually you are doing something not right, or unhealthy for you. it can be a negative generational tendency. your body is using pain as a message to get you to change. figure out the solution in the energetic world and then that will descend into the physical world. thats the way life works and the way energy flows...

tibetian sky burials

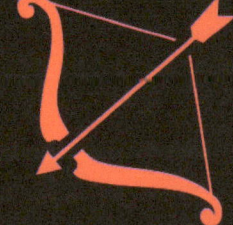

in tibet they have sky burials where you are left on a mountain to be consumed by vultures...

curse of the shamans

the curse of the shamans. 95% of the population of the tribal people were murdered by the church when they sent their missionaries to all the countries of the world. the shamans of those tribes before they were murdered placed the "curse of the shamans" on the conquerors. some examples: cocaine and chocolate of south america. tobacco of north america. alcohol of europe. sugar of india. salt of china. coffee of africa. these were all sacred alchemical ways before the church fucked with the Laws of Nature. now they are the alchemical chains that bind most of the population.
the curse of the shamans must be lifted before we will be free...

flowing going

go with the flow...

grounded

mega

thoth built all 83 000 megalithic structures over a 400 year period just before the sinking of atlantis. all of the megalithic structures including stonehenge, machu pichu, medicine wheels of north america and the pyramids in china, tibet and south america, to name a few, are all built upon a golden mean spiral that starts at the pyramids in egypt. this grid was built in an effort to protect the world from the darkness since the fall of atlantis...
~ drunvalo melchizedek - *the ancient secret of the flower of life*

when green was illegal

back in the 1600's you could be hanged for wearing green. it was the colour of the Faeries. the church was serious about wiping out all sources of magick!

pleiadian tales

"your health and well-being must be your choice. the dips in life, the so-called down times, are designed to buff you, to take you into the carwash or tune-up shop of life so you will come out shining and running again.
many of you experience great fear when your bodies malfunction remember the prisoners of anger that you hold in your

field? well, it is most important to cleanse your field and to be grateful for who you are, for that is one of the tests you were born to master.

   will you forget your lesson and be a grumbling victim holding a vibration that attracts more and more of its kind?
or will you trust the whispers of meaning, significance and purpose that are awakening in all of you?
what you do and think are connected to everything around you: the Earth, the animals, the weather.
you paint the landscape you experience day in and day out, so paint masterpieces of your lives, truly debunking limited thinking and fear as your only options in living."
~ barbara marciniak - *family of light*

underground

if you are ungrounded it means you are not in your body...
if you are not in your body then who or what is?

eyes of horus

self

we deal with war - but can we deal with our own self hatred?

free energy

there is more than enough energy in the world for us all with tidal, wave, solar, wind and geothermal alternative power sources. it is just that the secret government makes so much money on fossil fuels, our dependency and its scarcity, that they do not want to actually have fuel or energy that is environmentally friendly because they will lose out on profit...

Otherwise

Otherwise cannot create anything. it can only steal what has already been created.
pervert and manipulate it and then call it its own

old

the world is run by out-of-balance old men. no wonder it appears to suck...

wheaties

wheat is a drug. salt is a drug. sugar is a drug. caffeine is a drug. it is wise to not give your kids drugs.

snack

aliens eat emotions.

dark and light

light people are dynamic. airy and blissful. they do not attach to things as they pass through them. they can be uncaring and superficial. dark people are magnetic. they hold onto things. they can fester. overthinking. heavy. dense. messy. they tend to have things to work through because things easily attach to them...

crutch

where is the balance in human beings using technology as a crutch?

do it

exercise makes your body not hurt

mountains

where are the hermits in mountains?

reflect

i am a mirror

g

the art of balancing synthetic and organic tools together in tandem. the way to get it because of the way the Earth is. they both consist of elements. one is Creatrix born (creates no karma). and one is spelled by a magickian (creates karma)

to be human

humans are billions of years old. we did not evolve from monkeys. we were not genetically created by reptilian aliens. we originally had 12 strands of dna. some of us will have 12 strands of dna again with the coming apocalypse

i am

i work solo. i am not a part of any club, organization, society, religion, group. i am not affiliated with any one. i do not work for or with anyone. i do not follow any belief system other than my own. i do not follow any rules other than my own (as much as possible at least). i am witch. i worship Nature and the Laws of Nature. i worship Faeries and the elements. i worship the wind. i worship animals. i worship God and Goddess: the Creatrix. i worship me...

enuma elish

the old testament is a copy of a text called the enuma elish from sumer (a city that used to be in modern iraq) written in 4000 bc...

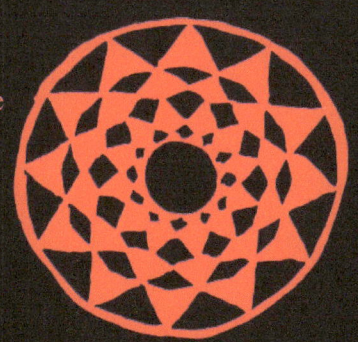

will you

there is nothing but hunting, following and reveling in your will...

anunnaki

the Fallen Angel anunnaki aliens came to Earth 450 000 years ago. they genetically altered the dna of humans. after the flood they taught man how to domesticate animals, agriculture, mathematics, writing, engineering, metallurgy, calendars, astrology, science... they then began the kingship of Earth. all royalty and american presidents descend from these aliens. they started insurance, banking, governments, police, the justice system, media... they try to control the world we live in. they are psychic parasites who use us as food. they need us more than we need them

their bloodline mingled with humans and created powerful hybrids that became:
yahweh, the creators of the pyramids, stonehenge, mermaids, dragons, serpents, snake of eden, goliath, Fallen Angels, illuminati, merovingians, great emperors of asia, nephilim of the bible, nagas of india, buddha, quetzalcoatl and the mayan calendar, olympiads of greece, noah and his descendants, cain and able, melchizedeks, the mystery schools, thoth, the pendragons, the tuatha de danaan, argartha and shamballa, pacal votan, jesus, dracula, the egyptian pharaohs, and natives from the americas and tribes from africa just to name a few...
there is no system on Earth that they do not control. (please pause and think about that for a minute...)

addiction

addiction is unhealthy. it will make you die faster and with more pain. avoid excess sugar, salt, fat, alcohol, cigarettes, pharmaceuticals, white vinegar, white flour. they create overproduction of mucous in the body. mucous traps all the nasty chemicals in our reality around the heart muscle. humans magick power is the ability to express love free of conditions from the heart. mucous stops humans from doing this. heart disease is the number one killer of humans.
i wonder, is there a connection there? (sarcasm)

e=o

chinese medicine correlation between emotions and organs... (liver = anger for example)

mind control

religion is a form of mind control. all religions come from the same manipulative source

Earth

the Earth is a sentient being, meaning she is alive. minerals, elements, plants, animals are alive!
talk to them! they can hear you and will respond. ask the tree what kind of tree it is, he will tell you!...

balance not duality

there is no such thing as black/white magick, evil/good or wrong/right. they are Fallen Angel false energetic constructs...

war

all wars are planned. economic troubles like recessions and depressions are planned by a small elite group of ultra rich men who own %99 of the worlds resources. they profit off of these things - that is why they create them. duh

illusionists

external authority figures and their experts are illusionists

imbalance

right now male energy is more predominant than female energy...

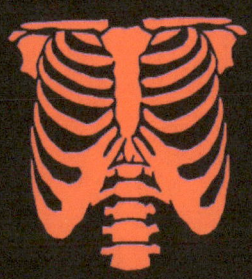

this unbalance in the force causes humans a lot of psychological stress

big pharma

pharmaceuticals are our biggest problem. they are keeping people alive when they should be dead. hence overpopulation. resources being held by old people who are out of touch and should be dead. the resources should be in the hands of the young in order to have a healthy younger generation (the future?) and to support change which is what will support the present static situation of disease of the world. over-population goes against the Laws of Nature.   Mother Nature created death to maintain the balance of life. humans are not intelligent enough to get involved!

trinity

horus   osiris   isis

the first family to ascend
being able to remember yourself
through the veil of death

~ drunvalo melchizedek

Earth Guardian

you are an Earth Guardian. a Guardian of the heart chakra of the Universe, planet Earth. a multidimensional being built to survive over a thousand years. meant to be full of bliss and happy. meant to be free of stress, worry, depression, anger, hatred. meant to be in perfect balance. meant to be free. meant to be vibrantly alive. meant to know, to care, to share...

exorcising

to exorcise Otherwise you must remain equanimous to it. meaning you must feel it to its full extent and be free of judgement. ignore it, do not give it any power and then it will disappear...

law of attraction

law of attraction works. what you believe is the truth. you will manifest what you believe

alchemy

humans are being controlled by the alchemy they consume. alchemy is the things you put in, on and around you. there are synthetic chemicals in food, artificial flavouring, make-up, perfume, beer, body soap, creams, hair products, laundry soap, cologne, building materials, air fresheners, meat containing antibiotics, polyester...
synthetic chemicals are neurotoxins.
that means it retards brain performance (makes you dumb) with prolonged exposure...

the law

"for every action is an equal and opposite reaction..." (love & light = hate & shadow)
~ newtons third law of motion

debt begone!

we do not have to live in a monetary system. we could live in a world without money

enough already

there is enough for everyone. there is enough money, food, drinking water, free energy, gasoline, oil and everything else for all of us. the things we need to live are abundant... (they are just be hoarded and controlled by the secret government)

greys

eisenhower made a deal with the grey aliens back in 1947.
give us your technology and you can abduct as many people as you want

media = mind control

mainstream media is controlled and censored by the Fallen Angels...

aura

strengthen your aura for vibrant health

no

negative protesting does not work. remember the star trek episode with that glowy thing that when they shot it, it would

just get bigger? your buying dollars are more powerful

Wheel of the Year

the Wheel of the Year calendar is real. it is a calendar based on the Earth and the Sun and the times of the equinoxes and the solstices. at those specific times the Earth opens and shares her energy with us. these holidays are to be celebrated on specific days. the church changed the days of those holidays so the natural cycle is perverted so we miss out on the energy the Earth wants to share with us. the church turned those sacred days into hallmark fests

out with ya

image producing machines kill the imaginations of humans...

giving

give your Moon blood or semen to the Earth, then she will know you and keep you safe

powa

you are powerful

authority ha ha

authority figures lie to get you to do what they want you to do

free will

Earth is a free will zone
- meaning anything goes

corporate america

corporate america funded hitler. george bush sr.'s standard oil, general electric, ford, wall st., federal reserve bank of new york, president franklin d. roosevelt's georgia warm springs foundation, general motors, du pont, union carbide, goodrich, westinghouse, gilette, singer, kodak, coca-cola, itt and the bank of england to name just a few... axis & allies = bullshit

gateway

"The Scarlet Woman as the representative of Nuit is the gateway to the Void..."
~ kenneth grant - *aleister crowley and the hidden god*

mmm

   merlin, merk and i (morgan) used to go down to where the pyramids would meet the water very early in the morning before the sun came up. the pyramids went into the water for many feet and so they created a nice smooth limestone almost like a water slide down into the water.
   there were many crocodiles there and we would go swimming with them. i remember being in that oily mineral water with my brothers, laughing and playing. my bothers hair would wrap around me in the dark.
   we spent hours lazing about this particular place because we loved to watch the blue lightning arc from the crocodiles over the surface of the water. we were able to dance and swim in this lightning and it would travel down our bodies invigorating us with its power.

we would fuck under the light of the full Moon as it illuminated the pyramids under us, bathing in divine blue lightning. the power of the lightning would go into our orgasms and they lasted for nights... the crocodiles eyes would blaze around us as their tails violently switched. sometimes the lightning would break out and go running over the sand dunes you could see far into the moonlight...

georgy porgy

george bushs first million was made with investment help from osama bin ladens older brother salem bin laden. he had invested lots of money into george bushs first company "arbusto energy" back in the 70's... weird coincidence (!?)

Earth

the Earth is over 5 billion years old and you think we need to save her?... i think you got it backwards...

frequency control

frequency control: the use of frequency (radio waves, microwaves, noise pollution, phone lines, cable lines, electricity...) to control the energy of humans by literally placing a net around them (frequency fence) that will not allow higher vibrations (light or information) to penetrate...

prophecy

there is a prophecy that says if the ravens leave the tower of london that the tower and great britain will crumble and the crown jewels would be lost. so the royals have clipped all the ravens wings... (you cannot keep forever what is not yours)

china olympics

the slogan of the chinese olympic games: "one world - one dream." china has murdered about 2.5 million innocent people with war. who knows why they are so pissed at tibetian monks. what i do not understand is why the world is going to support such crimes by having this great big party called the olympics in beijing. china murderer of millions! lets go dump billions of dollars in support of them and celebrate the new world orders "one world one dream" what a bunch of horse crap...

mass

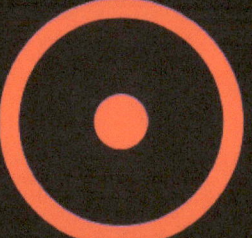

i do not celebrate mass for christ

illuminati

   "the illuminati, the clique which control the direction of the world, are genetic hybrids, the result of interbreeding between a reptilian extraterrestrial race and humanity many thousands of years ago. the centre of power is not even in this dimension -- it is in the lower fourth dimension, the lower astral as many people call it, the traditional home for the "Demons" of folklore and myth. these fourth-dimensional reptilian entities work through these hybrid bloodlines because they have a vibrational compatibility with each other. this is why the european royal and aristocratic families have interbred so obsessively, as do the so-called eastern establishment families of the united states, which produce the leaders of america. every presidential election since and including george washington in 1789 has been won by the candidate with the most european royal genes. of the 42 presidents to bill clinton, 33 have been genetically related to two people, alfred the great, king of england, and charlemagne, the most famous monarch of what we now call france.
it is the same wherever you look in the positions of power... they are the same tribe!"
~ david icke - *the biggest secret*

rape of the Goddess

you cut her down once a year. prop her up in your house. decorate her like a harlot for cheap thrills for a few weeks. then throw her on the side of the street like a used whore. this is how you treat Mother Nature when you celebrate mass for christ... millions of trees killed. each tree takes 15 years to grow. love trees by celebrating their life - not their death. not to mention the trees cut down for wrapping paper and cards that are casually throw out after a few short weeks...

ascension

there was a quarantine placed upon the Earth about 13 000 years ago - so there has been no where to ascend to for a long time now... (meaning modern "ascended masters" are lying to you...)
~ drunvalo melchizedek - *the ancient secret of the flower of life*

life is simple

life is real fucking simple: fear............................love

corp

corporation = corporatio = assuming a body = not of the Earth = alien = corporations = consumers = slavery

path of the Dragon

ley lines are the energy pathways of the Dragon in the center of the Earth as she flies around the planet. she is Goddess. avebury in england is the largest, with 12 ley lines intersecting. it is the largest megalithic structure with almost 100 sarsen stones (like stonehenge). it is also the heart chakra of the planet. there use to be megalithic structures, sarsen stones, sacred springs or a huge sacred tree at each ley line crossing. until the church destroyed most of them...

in the moment

in the moment, i want to own who i am - and not be a synthetic replica of myself...

conspiracy

   "conspiracy theory" this is a label ignorant people give to any information that irritates their ignorance. it is a sweeping statement made so the person is free from having to actually do any research in an effort to learn about the true nature of reality. typically the person who uses this statement is unable to think for themselves and simply accepts societal norms they are told as truth...
   this person usually still trusts the authority figures of society and does not believe they are lying in an effort to control, manipulate and profit off the terror of the general public. there is no point in communicating with them because they are still in their walled cocoon and unable to see the truth even if it smacked them in the face. they are pod people. they are asleep. they still buy into the matrix. any threat to their understanding of the matrix is scary and troubling for them, for it is all they have...
   see the mysteries cannot be taught, they can only be experienced. there is no proof. for how can you prove when you feel love? belief cannot be measured with the rational mind, it can only be measured with the heart and the soul. when you ask for proof you are using the wrong tools for the job. so those who are still in the cocoon of the unbeliever, the zombies, the walking dead, when they stare at the ceiling and demand to know what you are so damn happy about - just nod and smile as you enjoy the stars above...

cancer sucks ass

cancer eats our tender flesh as a sign that something is not right in the force...

apathy

if we really were existing in the true nature of reality would there be so much conflict? nature is perfect with her seeds, flowers, growth, death... what man builds is inherently flawed. thats why theres war, rules, politics, structure, murder... humans can be stupid because we follow the leader. and do what we are told (well most of us at least). living for the quick fix of bliss from outside of ourselves. the collective apathy is pathetic and so we live pathetically...

misguided fallen Angels

   the Fallen Angels actually spliced their 11 stranded dna into 10 stranded dna in an effort to get away from the Agents of the 13th dimension (Sacred Law - corrections) that were chasing them across the Universe. they actually created a plane of existence that she did not birth in (the illusion of hell). they intentionally de-evolved themselves and then came to Earth the gateway in the Sun. they threw an electronic frequency fence (a net) around Earth to cut us humans off from the Creatrix in order to feed off of us and harvest our energy.
   in effect de-evolving us as well, but without our permission. the thing is now they have become addicted to us and gold. but there is this thing called the apocalypse coming. which means that the Creatrix is helping us re-evolve back to our original place (Paradise). but those Fallen Angels cannot come because they have no souls! heres the catch: you can only

survive the apocalypse if you have a soul! so the silly Fallen Angels have totally caught themselves in their own net because we are outta here (the illusion of hell) and they cannot follow!...

merlin

merlin stole the Holy Grail from avalon and gave it to jesus who was passing by on his world sabbatical. jesus and joseph spent time on avalon learning the sacred mysteries from our priestesses. merlin did this so the grail would become a beacon of light in the coming dark age of christian dictatorship... the Holy Grail has always called to the ones with magick in their hearts. we owe merlin our thanx...

vitriol

v.i.t.r.i.o.l. visita interiora terrae rectificando invenies occultum lapidem.
visit the interior parts of the Earth by rectification thou shalt find the hidden stone...

faerieland

exterminating Angels

exterminating Angels. here on Earth because when the shift comes so many people will die so quickly that the Death

Walkers have marked you with your destination just to keep things running smoothly through the gates of death...

mars

we should give mars back to the martians and tell them to go there and leaves us alone...

starfire

"...the scarlet women were so called because of their being a direct source of the priestly star fire. they were known in greek as the hierodulai (sacred women) - a word later transformed (via medieval french into english) to 'harlot.' in the early germanic tongue they were known as horês, which was later anglicised to 'whores.' however, the word originally meant, quite simply, 'beloved ones.' as explained in good etymological dictionaries, these words were descriptions of high veneration and were never interchangeable with such definitions as prostitute or adulteress. their now common association was, in fact, a wholly contrived strategy of the medieval roman church in its bid to denigrate the noble status of the sacred priestess…"
~ laurence gardner - *genesis of the grail kings*

new years 1999

new years 1999. the queen of england was going to light the river thames on fire with a four hundred foot wall of flame. a flaming serpent which just happened to point exactly east to the pyramids in egypt where the illuminati were planning to put a gold capstone on the pyramid. it was all timed for midnight 2000 greenwich mean time.

fortunately for us the lizard queen was unable to get her wall of flame lit on time and the lizards priests ceremony with the capstone was canceled because they could not get the capstone to fit. they were trying to perform these Otherwise magick ceremonies to open a portal for more Otherwise energies to flood into the Earth dimension.

just imagine looking from space at a large flaming arrow pointing to a golden portal opening at the pyramids. the priests in egypt were planning on using the pink floyd crowd (pink floyd were playing at the pyramids that new years) as a battery because the people were really high and just oozing their energy everywhere. they were also using the global fear of y2k. its easy for Fallen Angels to come along and scoop up human energy and fear up and use it as the fuel like a battery for their nasty rituals...
~ david icke - from his website - "call to all lightworkers!"

lords and ladies of fuck-all

the lords and ladies of fuck-all. are all dressed up for the ball. for even they have heard the call. with diamonds and gold. for which their souls they have sold

feelings nothing more than feelings

falling into despair, anger and upset feelings is exactly where the Fallen Angels want you to be. then they can feed off your angst...

sodom & gomorrah

it was an explosion from a nuclear weapon that wiped out sodom and gomorrah, not "god"...

white powder

when they first broke into the great pyramid they found a pile of white powder in the sarcophagus in the middle of the kings chamber. they bottled it, it is still in the british museum. scientific analysis revealed that it is the crystallized excretions from thousands of pineal glands...

~ drunvalo melchizedek - *the ancient secret of the flower of life*

within

everything is within. (and i mean literally)...

youre the one

there is one family who own over 96% of the worlds resources

trinity

hiya. i am trinity. i am the only one like me. i am in perfect balance!... i am the bellybutton of the Universe...

zombies

can you imagine if you could not buy cigarettes, weed, alcohol, cocaine, pot, sugar, meth, gas, porn, heroin, crack? the streets would be filled with fucked up freaking out zombies... do you know one person who is not addicted to anything?

names

the holy roman church did not even decide upon the name jesus christ (they called him a whole bunch of other things) until 14th century...
thats 1400 years after the supposed crucification of christ...

gregorian

new years is part of the gregorian calendar. you know the calendar decreed by pope gregory XIII out of the vatican in 1582? ha ha suckered in by christian dogma again...

flavour fla

artificial flavouring = synthetic = petrochemicals = gas. strange how a lot of food at the grocery store contains crude oil...

why

poison has somehow been accepted by humans as sustenance...

666

there are 666 female ley lines crossings on planet Earth…

seed

down in the center of the Earth. down in the iron core crystal. down in the magnetic heartbeat of Mother Earth. lies an orb. this seed is one cell. the one perfect cell of the Paradise. the original state of Earth. the holographic theory states that you only need one cell to manifest the whole. so this orb is a perfect miniature replica of Paradise. perfectly sealed, impenetrable and awaiting the right time. a seed...

really high on e

when youre really high on e and your talking so much and sharing so much, where does all that energy go? what if there are reptilian Fallen Angels called anunnaki who live in the 4th dimension which is your imagination. what if their dinner is your colourful energy? maybe thats where all that energy goes...

be your own brand

the quest for the Holy Grail is real. all our imaginary heroes and villains are coming true. our imaginations are coming alive all around us. have you noticed people are a little kooky these days? the legend says that arthur and merlin were killed and the Holy Grail disappeared. the Holy Grail is real, and arthur and merlin still are alive. they were just waiting. waiting for now. magicians are alive. and in fact, you are one too. magick is real. your imagination is real.
you just have to imagine yourself as a character and then become it. you have to become that character with costume and sound, props and even an accent. actually become your imagination. but be your own brand. be yourself.
its now or never. i mean its not going to get better unless we make it better. someone else isnt going to save the fucking world. you are...

orgasm

massive deep sacred orgasmic wave fields

fuck

psychiatry has murdered more people than all the wars combined...

laws

not only is it the laws that are so fucked. its all the chickenshits who
follow them and tattle-tale on others thats the problem as well (rats)

bible

what the bible writers do not want you to know is that the holy spirit in
history always referred to sophia - wisdom - the mother of God...

proof is in the puddin

the system is not working...

equal?

we are all equal? thats bullshit. every soul is a different age.
some are Onceborns, some are Firstborns, and some are somewhere in between…

missing link my ass

missing link? there is a huge gap between the so called 'evolution' between homo erectus and homo sapien. like millions years of evolution that does not have support in the fossil records. scientist try to tell you that we evolved from monkeys - how insulting. why are there still monkeys then? Fallen Angels who were master geneticists landed and genetically spliced our dna and added the reptilian part of our brain making us more like them...
unlike the missing link, there is plenty of evidence for this phenomena...

age of unenlightenment

the roman catholic church burned millions of women at the stake during the inquisition. women who were midwives, wisewomen, herbalists and folk doctors. the ones who birthed the babies and the ones who helped the old ones die. the givers of life and death. coincidently the black plague struck and killed two-thirds the population of the European continent. smart that eh!?

   they took the power of healing from the women and gave it to men who started modern medicine and called it the "age of enlightenment." enlightenment does not come from a foundation of stolen power, murder and lies...

free and flaming star

"...like the Beast, The Scarlet Woman is feared by the church for good reason. after being driven into a role of servitude and shame for centuries, she is about to be recognized as a free and flaming star..."
~ james donahue

common sense

bush senior, colin powell and norman schwarzkopf all got knighted by the queen after the iraqi war.   the u.s.a. went through a war in order to be free of britian (many deaths). so why are your leaders kneeling down in front of the queen?

paradox

today the churches are still covered in gold and gems while the population mainly starves. humans have to now pay for healthcare that makes people sick, food that makes people hungry, water that is dirty, clothes that are poisonous, pay taxes to rich landowners. where is the sense in that?

oh no

expectations only lead to disappointment...

fuck recession

funny how the word recession is on the lips of everyone and yet how much profit did the stores and corporations make in the last few weeks (x-mas holidays)? because humans feel buying presents is how to show love?
funny how the way we celebrate and show love is actually hurting humans, animals and our planet...

faerie

   a Faerie? what is a Faerie, Fey, Fairy, Fay? a Faerie is a spirit. every element has a spirit, just like every human has a spirit. a spirit is the soul or essence of something. even machines and houses or buildings have souls. everything is made of elements. everything has its own Faerie. a rock has its own Faerie, a tree has its own Faerie, a pond has its own Faerie, carrots have their own Faerie, metals have their own Fairies. radiation has its own Fairies.

   uranium, iron, gold, hydrogen, carbon, mercury, silica and all the elements each have their own Faerie. so with uranium for example, uranium has a natural place of existence. i mean uranium lives in the ground. thats where its home is, thats where it is happy. a long time ago people decided to take uranium and other elements from their homes out of the ground and bring them to the surface of the planet and use them because they have lots of energy.

   thereby we have machines, factories, and gasoline for example to run our world. fossil fuels run our world. the only problem is that the fairies of the elements that have been translocated are not happy. we did not ask their permission to move them or use them in this fashion. they have been removed from their homes and they are pissed off.

   so what happens when a Faerie, the spirit of the element, gets angry? they become Demons. Demons are angry Faeries unfortunately an angry uranium Demon has quite a bit of force. so lets say that angry uranium Demon gets displaced and somehow a human ends up swallowing it. now this tiny little chemical is in the system of the human. the Faerie is stuck in the guts of a human. it is kinda like the fairies home, warm, squishy, active. but the Faerie is smarter than the human because it is still in the hand of the Goddess, and it knows the human can hear it, so it starts to scream. i want to go home! the human probably cant hear the voice of the little Faerie, but the soul of the human does.

so what happens? the angry Faerie/Demon causes itself to vibrate. the element of uranium starts to vibrate and the human develops malignant cells causing cancer. the end result is the human dies and the Faerie gets what it wants which is to be returned to the Earth through the process of decomposition.

if you are aware, you can do meditations and ask the spirits, elementals, Faeries to leave your body. you can release the Faeries back to the Earth. "if there are spirits in my body, negative thought forms, Faeries or the like i recognize your existence and i want to assist you to return back home to the Earth. please come into my hand so i can release you." open an energetic vortex to the centre of the Earth and drop them in. make sure to close the vortex. and say thank you Goddess

you might be surprised at the voices in your head. you can always offer them something as well, kind of like a goodwill gesture. Faeries love presents and will usually respond to an offering. i am in service to the Faeries and this is our way. we do not mean to harm you humans but we would like to return home. and our Mother Earth to return to the place of balance and harmony...

Earth is a venus fly trap

3rd dimensional Earth once you are in you cannot get out unless you have a soul!...

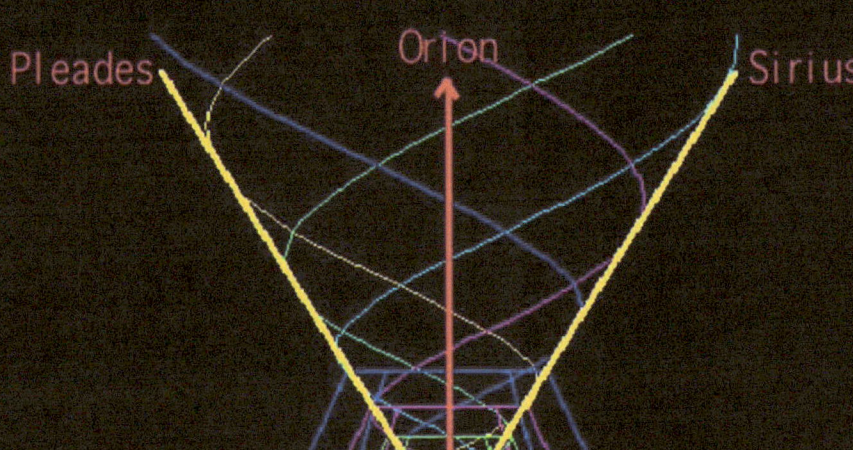

Earth →

~ pic from dan winter

where are you going?

when the apocalypse comes and the Earth experiences a dimensional shift, you might notice objects appearing. they are not from our dimension so do not touch them! they could suck you into a place you do not want to go...

collective unconscious

collective unconscious. where all of our imaginations are linked. represented by the dreams, aspirations, memories, imaginations and myths of humans and Faerie Tales. we are all connected. i mean just think of waste treatment plants where all our vital essences mingle and become one...

old men

i understand that the founding fathers of your country ran away from england to form a nation that was based on 'freedom from oppression.' but when you look at the u.s.a. today it is the most heavily controlled police state in the world (especially after 911). you minds are controlled by the media that is run by a handful of old men. your relationships are controlled by a social structure that has been created by a handful of old men. your belief systems are controlled by religion that was made by a handful of old men. your consumerism is controlled by the economic system created by a handful of old men. your leadership is controlled by a political system made by a handful of old men. where is your freedom now?

robert morning star

in 1947 a spaceship crashed in the southern states and a group of hopi natives rescued a little grey being they named star elder. they hid him from the government while this little grey being taught the hopi elders what he knew about the history of Earth, the visitation of aliens to planet Earth for centuries, some of his technology etc. this group of hopi natives gathered a group of hopi children that were taught by this little grey man. they were taught many incredible things including running 6 miles with a mouth full of water without spilling a drop, and with their backs turned and catching arrows out of the air. one of those childrens grandson is named robert morning star who tours the united states speaking of his grandfathers experiences with star elder...
~ robert morning star - *the terra papers*

memory is subjective

when you study the burning times, you will notice that the actual number of women burned at the stake by the church seem to miraculously go down every year...

Harvestin

God dies in the fall and his spirit enters into the harvest so we all may eat and live another year...

tingle

whatever jingles your bells...

blue

blue reptilian metallic hominoids or bluebloods...

how to become a faerie

master Faerie craftsmen. craftsmen who are so good at their craft that they became legendary because of the quality of the construction of things they make. and those legends survive the passing time. they became known this way because of the time and loving energy spent and the power of their elemental Earth manipulations, eventually becoming a Faerie Tale.

vatican controls history

christians possess the world and sometimes it seems our holidays are just based on their dogma. but those holidays have older origins. Winter Solstice or Yule. the longest night of the year. light a fire in the Sun Gods honour. there are over eighty similarities with jesus of the christian stories and a pagan Sun God that existed thousands of years before christianity.

the christians stole their mythology from the tribes that they conquered. the winners always write the history books. the history books all start at year 0. we are told there wasnt writing before then. there were books that existed before the year 0 and they are in the vaults underneath the vatican. if you control the books you can control how people think. we as humans give our power away to the Fallen Angel systems when we worship false idols

polar shift

there is something called a polar shift. its happened many many times throughout the herstory of the Earth. the magnetic pole literally switch and can move location. when this happens the Earth magnetic fields drops to nothing. humans memories are held in the physical body with magnetics. so when the Earth loses her magnetic field - humans lose their memories. so humans have been on Earth for billions of years, its just that we can lose our memories when we experience a polar shift. so we have forgotten how long we have been here for.

instead we tend to believe the Fallen Angels bullshit shoved down our throats, like they were the ones who made us. there are ways to make it with your memory intact through a pole shift. humans have something called a merkaba:

it is a vehicle of light that each human has.
   when your merkaba is activated it will keep your memory intact while traveling through a polar shift... its your choice whether you die or survive the upcoming changes.
~ gregg braden - "awakening to zero point"

guilt trip

humans are not responsible for the destruction of the Earth. it is just an Fallen Angel guilt trip

girt with sword

Moon

following the phases of the Moon changes your life...

photons

basically the amount of photons from the center of the Universe is increasing (shift). these photons (immensely concentrated units of light) raise the vibration of the Earth and everything on it. this is a natural cleansing the Earth experiences. in their presence lower vibrations simply cannot exist. the vibration of Earth is starting to accelerate so you will find that if you experiencing lower vibrational emotions or are participating in lower vibrational actions, pain will be the end result. vibration is equal to energy.

so if you eat processed foods, smoke cigarettes and drink alcohol, your body will have a more difficult time withstanding intense amounts of energy... whereas if you are conscious of what you put in your body, spend time outdoors, and are really active, your body will be more likely to be able to withstand higher vibrational energies...

giants

the liquid metallic reptilian Fallen Angel aliens who came to Earth. about 450 000 years ago eventually figured out a way to mate with humans. these offspring became the giants of in the bible. these hybrids were really big, had super strength, lived long. they were the heroes of old (hercules, gilgamesh, noah). that is why things like the pyramids, stone circles, ziggurats, stone temples are so big because they were made by giants...

vatican secrets

ever wonder what is in the 85 kilometers of vatican secret archives?

alchemical war

there is an alchemical war going on. this means your mind is being controlled by the alchemy you consume. your brain functions with neurotransmitters, the fuel for neurotransmitters is nutrients. most of the food out there has little or no actual value to your body because it is so low in nutrients.

not to mention 1-methylcyclopropene, artificial colours, artificial flavoring, aspartame, astaxanthin, benzoic acid/sodium benzoate, bha and bht, canthaxanthin, emulsifiers, high-fructose corn syrup, msg, olestra, partially-hydrogenated oils, potassium bromate and nitrates. avoid these at all costs.

sugar, caffeine, alcohol, fat, tobacco are addictive drugs and are killing you. they are also keeping you docile as you line up for the slaughter. if you eat a lot of these things over time your body actually loses its ability to digest real food properly. find real food!

the power of blood

when women live together they start to bleed at the same time. in the old days at that time of the month woman would gather in Moon lodges where they would sit and bleed into the ground. women would exchange blood for power with Mother Earth.
men were not allowed near the Moon lodge or women when they were bleeding. women were held in awe and worshiped as goddesses because we could bleed and not die. something men cannot do. there were groups of male priests that would cut their balls and penis off to mimic the power of women. lets celebrate the return of the moon lodges!...

tree

love attitude work

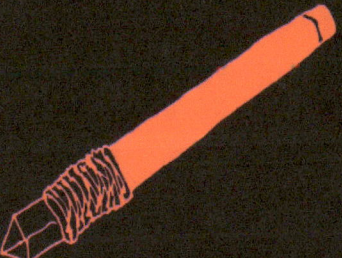

censorship sucks

there are no words to describe how offensive the censorship is on facebook. nudity, ritual, sex, sacred alchemy, and rock n roll are my religion. and they have no right to censor what i post. for all the amazing art that makes it on my wall, there is an equal amount i have to pass by because i am "not allowed" to post it because of the "threat" of being "blocked" by the fb nazis. facebook is a perfect example of the insidious nature of control upon planet Earth and her beautiful humans. but they have no problem shoving their fucking christ x-mas songs down my throat when i leave my house, like they have a right to do so. like they have a right to bombard with their stupid advertising. like they have the right to take away my free will! karma will always make you pay. for every action has an equal and opposite reaction. and the time has come...

the watchtower

i have hidden and hid so they wouldnt find me. a thousand times over have they killed me. a thousand times over i have escaped. the hunted now chase the hunter. yes they listen for me even now, so if as a little mouse i squeak do they turn their sharp hearing, their keen eyes. they are only machines. but the puppets have masters and those masters use a watchtower, a lighthouse to listen with. to sense, sending out its listening light ray. an angry powerless ghost

witches we are

humans burned at the stake the church took our property, jewles, livestock, possessions souls... we will have them back

five

five: the pentagram has five points, five senses, five platonic solids (sacred geometry universal building blocks), five fingers, the elliptical path of venus forms a perfect pentagram, flowers have five petals, the golden ratio, starfish, five planets visible with the naked eye, tongue can experience five tastes, aleister crowley said every man and every woman is a star...

supreme elixir

"sole source of supreme elixir = the virgin whore of heaven who sheds her star light without direct sexual contact"
~ kenneth grant

Holy Grail

"were these intrusions of the Grail into our inquiry, and others like them, merely random and coincidental? or was there a continuity underlying and connecting them - a continuity which, in some unimaginable way, did link our inquiry to the Grail, whatever the Grail might really be? at this point, we were confronted by a staggering question. could the Grail be something more than pure fantasy? could it actually have existed in some sense? could there really have been such a thing as the Holy Grail? or something concrete, at any rate, for which the Holy Grail was employed as a symbol?"
~ michael baigent, richard leigh & henry lincoln - *the holy blood and the holy grail*

build

all buildings should be built like roses...

why?

and the faerie asked
why do humans desecrate the holy temple?

walt way

the walt disney way. well the proof is plain to see, the way of walt disney does not work. britney a mouseketeer went through quite a rough patch and the media should be ashamed of how they condemned that girl, burnt just like a witch of old. you made her into your whore and now you sit back and ridicule her with your little nasty jokes. walt disney had a vision. it was believed in so much that the vision became real to the touch. well britney was one of walts girls and he has led her down the garden path. fame and riches do not make Angels. your michael jacksons and oj simpsons are a perversion of nature because you made them that way.

   most of the population is sitting on its ass laughing and pointing fingers, while your country is killing people in another land. but that is not enough because now you turn on yourself and start to munch on your own tail. walt and his way became a land, then a world, now it is a town. the way of celebration usa is horrifying. the judgement, the screening, the control, the brainwashing is really spooky.

   but it is not as scary as how easily you give away your free will to corporations. the corporations feed off of you like little batteries. did you ever wonder why britney freaked out and shaved her hair off? walt made britney and now who suffers the consequences of stealing, raping, pillaging, harvesting maiden female energy?

   you may laugh and snicker behind your chip greased little fingers but the joke is on you because britney spears is one of the most powerful witches you have got and she is the general of a vast army that you may think is only concerned with fun, but you are messing with girl power.

   britney spears, michael jackson, madonna and all of your synthetic Angels are trying to send you a message. maybe they do not want to be worshiped. maybe they want you to wake up and stop the war. you put them on a pedestal, but really your world is dying. look at what happened in louisiana with the flood. that could happen to you. and you do not have the resources to deal with crisis.   but you certainly have billions to sink into the academy awards or the war in iraq. like it means something.

   luxury is an illusion. there are not infinite resources to match your infinite hunger. what happens when the resources run out? how will you feed yourself then? it is not a joke. the system of the man is trying to keep you sedated with consumerism. it wants you to not be aware of the death all around you. it is your own death. can you smell yourself dying? because i can ya stinkers

akashic records

the akashic records of humans held in a magnetic band around the iron core crystal, at the center of the Earth.
all the records, of all the reincarnational lifetimes, of all the living beings that ever were...

ug

you want to hang out and talk with someone but their breath is too strong (dont forget to brush your teeth!)

forget it

information that is telling you that humans are weak, sick, by-product of aliens poo, lesser than, shit, sinners, created the evil, are responsible for the evil, made the hole in the ozone... no. nope. forget it. dont buy the lies of the Fallen Angels...

beez

beepollen is good for allergies

spinning

information spin is in everything

leave those boobs alone!

man-made boobs become aggressive titties. the Goddess makes better breasts than men ever could!

dont try - just do

be aware of your posture throughout the day

odds are

odds are if you are fat you have a gluten allergy...
(avoid wheat, sugar and dairy and you wont be fat anymore lazypants!)...

gee

exercising and work are two entirely different things...

Guardian of the Void

the Dark Goddess is the Guardian of the Void, the Mistress of Death, the Administrator of the Book of Souls and the Guardian of the Gate.

power

its about finding your personal power...

lost

some people are lost in the tunnels of set and do not know it...

before

everyone was tall, had strong bones and teeth and was disease free until you hit the time of agriculture. then everyone shrank, their bones got brittle, their teeth fell out and they were disease ridden...

pyramids

the pyramids were built over thirteen thousand years ago. they have moved less than a quarter of an inch...

bliss

the best way to be blissful is by making others blissful...

altar

your body is her altar. your elements are her temple. your blood is her holy wine...

scarab

the scarab beetle was worshiped because it laid its eggs in dung, so was thought to be holy because it created life out of nothing. he represents initiation. when you are in the darkest of places, carry your central sun (your goal) in front of you. let its light guide you through your darkness until it is over...

curly

i was at a party once talking to this really nice man, when i looked down and noticed he was wearing curly shoes. i looked up, surprised, but he was gone...

queens and princesses

"...without these queens and princesses, none of the kings associated with them throughout history would have been fit to reign. it is only she who can bestow the gift that brings sovereignty which as transcendence and creativity, bestows blessing and fertility upon the kingdom through a wisdom and depth of vision that anticipates difficulty and initiates productivity through activity that, for any other than the king and queen, would appear totally uncausative.

through the ability to see situations several steps down the line, they are able to plan ahead and bring blessing upon the land and the people. for this reason patriarchal religions hate women, like little boys trying to be free of mummys apron strings they deride the female for her authority.

the church is fully aware of the regal identity of the dragon kings and fully aware of the power of the grail princesses through whom and by whom those kings reigned.

for this reason the inquisition was particularly directed against specific females. puffed up with male pride and misogyny the church fully knew and hated the fact that beneath the symbol of the lamia lay the truth of a distinct neurological difference between not only fairy women, but fairy men as well. the dragon princesses produced a chemical that acted on their own physiology to produce a state of mental composure and grace that history symbolized as the swan, not only because of their elegance, but also to denote the origin in the anatomy of that chemical.

the consequent state of grace produced by this chemical and the energy it afforded, uninhibited or wasted by any preoccupation with stress or inner conflict, appeared to make the female glow with an inner serenity and beauty that many people described as fairy fascination.

the state of peace that they enjoyed was, to an ordinary care worn observer, utterly alluring and charming, a quality to adore because in proximity to her the energy could be felt like soft electricity which had a calmative affect on the mind which as it slowed down and became still began to perceive the joy and sense of oneness that has no beginning, no cause and no ending but lies hidden behind the internal barriers, taboos, fears and attachments that we use all our mental energy to sustain in our minds which, usually quite exhausted has no energy to spare to see beyond the tired struggle with imposed illusions.

in her company the observer would partake of her abundant morphic energy which could provide the observer with enough energy to see beyond and begin to understand that mortal care is unimportant. mind thus stilled glimpses the eternal and this is one aspect of hierogamy and the love that is death. the chemical also has a physical affect in transferred to the observer. the same stillness occurs and produces psychotropic effects.

the problem was though that the observer would have to have sufficient numbers of the correct axon membranes in the right type of synaptic receptors and an increased number of dendrites connecting the appropriate brain cells across both hemispheres. in other words the dragon princess had round pegs and dragon kings had lots of round holes, in contrast to non dragons, who seemed to have different shaped pegs and holes and less of either..."
~nicholas de vere – *the dragon legacy*

a bet

when i was in grade two a kid bet me i couldnt take a straight pin out of an electrical outlet. i won the bet, but i did get blown across the room during story time, caught the wall on fire and made all the kids cry.
i had a feeling i was different early on...

define

how do you define your will?

beaming

the beam of your focus makes anything it touches grow - and anything it ignores, disappear...

wegggie

humans cannot digest the cellulose in plants!...(therefore it is not a sufficient meat replacement)

food

food is a vibrational experience. i would rather be wild and randy like a buffalo than be meek and quiet like a carrot...

sarsen

sarsen stones. they store all the energy of all the magick of all the years. like here in north america there are thousands of medicine wheels left from the natives. haunting and beautiful in their own way...

sometimes you get called

i was hired by a magickian to come and be a watcher for his ceremonial work. we flew to england. he was going to do ceremony at st. michaels on the tor. that was a very strange night. we were followed by a mentally challenged man from the town of glastonbury down below. he appeared right after we were done ceremony around four in the morning.

he played the bagpipes. he took something i loved and turned it into something i didnt recognize. instantly my hackles rose. he asked to go down to his truck to have a cup of tea. it was my choice, and i heard the voice in my mind warn me, but i also knew it was what needed to be done.

for my whole being started to vibrate and i knew there was a god-spell upon us. for tea we went and this man was so strange. he didnt make sense when he spoke and he procured very strange feelings inside of me.

we ended up sleeping there for a few short hours. when i woke up i have never experienced that much pain before in my life. it felt as if my life essence was being drained. we walked down to the white spring, a magick shop at the foot of the tor where we met the owner. he started to talk with the magickian and i.

oddly enough he started telling us this experience he and his wife had had while traveling in switzerland. we couldnt believe our ears because it is exactly what had happened to us just last night. except for this couple started to be chased by a black helicopter and these people with no auras had put a strange compulsion upon them so it was so difficult for them to get away.

this man told us that they had implanted what was known as a "beacon" in lightworkers. a beacon to place a call around that magick worker so they were known to alien intelligence. the magickian immediately turned to me and looked me in the eye. are you okay?

at that time i was hardly able to stand i was in so much pain. he had special medicine which he called upon. he grabbed at my third chakra and with a twisting motion pulled black spaghetti out of my body.

it was squiggling in his hand. i almost threw up. he threw it to the ground where he had created a vortex down to the Goddess. he kept cleaning me out, throwing black morbid noodles into the ground, and quickly closed the vortex. i immediately felt myself again. later that night i ended up pulling the same shit out of his left shoulder with my crystal wands and another vortex down to the Goddess.

it was more difficult to get out than mine because it had all day to grow. i know now that that strange man had used some kind of spear in my back that had implanted an alien beacon in my centre and on the magickians left shoulder. i learned that megalithic structures are guarded and to be wary of those who do not seem right in the head...

34?

34 out of 44 u.s. presidents related by blood?!...

funny

funny how we project what we do not like about ourselves onto others...

acceptance

we should just shut up and accept each other already...

an immortal

you are an immortal...

harmonic temples

when they built the temples in egypt, they built them according to harmonic proportions and sacred geometry. they did not contain any corners and were therefore piezoelectric. in other words they were alive and still are...
~ john anthony west - "magical egypt"

horus

oh and by the way, there is no horusy doom here. in fact, i feel the exact opposite. because i believe we are superheros who have been slipped a sleeping potion and are just awakening in the garden of Paradise... yay! we made it!...

past

i remember my past lives and am writing a trilogy about them...

paradox

ignorance is a paradox because you dont realize you are in it...

huh

they found bones of modern homo sapiens deep in gold mines in africa that were 300 000 years old...
~ drunvalo melchizedek - *the ancient secret of the flower of life*

39

non-organic strawberries can have 39 separate applications of pesticides. just to name one of the many chemicals they are exposed to. pesticides are what directly cause cancer...

trapped

what the Fallen Angels did not realize when they caused the Fall from Paradise, is that Earth is a venus fly trap. and now they cannot get out! and with the upcoming shift they are really fucked because the only ticket out is a soul - something the Fallen Angels lost a long time ago!...

tiamat

"know that tiamat seeks ever to rise to the stars, and when the upper is united to the lower, then a new age will come of Earth, and the serpent shall be made whole, and the waters will be as one..."
~ the mad arab - *necrimonicon*

rainbow

magick is like a rainbow between a blue sky and a dark cloud. it all depends on how you look at it. how you hold your head. if you have your back to it you wont see it. if you dont look up you wont see it. if you dont care you wont see it what the fuck is a rainbow anyway?

cat to but

a caterpillar completely liquefies in order to become a butterfly...

easy peasy

to love the Earth is an easy choice...

for real

virgin princess...

presidents

all 43 presidents have had european royal blood and all european royalty are related as well. 34 presidents descend from one guy - charlemagne. presidents are not chosen by ballot, they are chosen by bloodline. bush is related to the queen of england and to bill clinton, john kerry, al gore, bob dole, his wife barbara. one of bushes ancestors led the crusades in freeing jerusalem from the islamic faith. bushes words of a 'crusade' against 'islamic' terrorism are exactly charlemagnes words in his crusade against the muslims... so if america declared independence from europe in 1776 then why are all the u.s. presidents from european bloodlines?

Goddess Grail

satan?

   do you not get it? there is no such thing as hell, satan, satanism. the church made it all up in order to scare people into going to church. they used to charge people money to enter their places of worship. they made a killing off of satan satanism is making fun of the blind ignorance of the people who believe in satan dumbass!
   its a joke! a joke in the face of the church. the only way to believe in satan is if your christian. get it? i am not a christian. i do not believe in their god or their satan. they made it all up! there is no such place as hell. there is no such place as heaven. its all a bunch of brainwashing the nicene council decided on in constantinople in 325 ad. their political agenda propagated using the media. the romans are Fallen Angels. they choose christianity to be their banner. they decided to take over the world with straight lines. straight lines do not exist in nature. romans are aliens!
   they created the system. the system is straight lines: streets, telephone lines, time, money, birth to death. straight lines are alien! the system is hell. the Fallen Angels are intentionally creating the illusion of hell here on Earth. an evil spell the romans are putting on us trying to get us to believe in their visions of hell.

but it is just an illusion. you can pierce the illusion. look beyond the straight line… the fibonacci sequence is the spiral of life. everything grows according to the fibonacci sequence.   they turned the Goddess into satan. they turned her consort The Horned One into the devil. the concepts are our human heritage that are billions of years old. they want you to believe in the last two thousand years. we have been here for more than four billion years!

satan is not the issue. they are sucking your pineal glands, your heart and your blood. that is the issue. Earth is Paradise of the Universe. the pollution and damage is not the fault of the humans. it is the Fallen Angels who are intentionally messing things up trying to recreate their home life. they really want you to believe in hell: duality, murder, rape, stealing, aggression, hate, jealousy, perversions, gluttony, war. these are alien concepts to humans. we would never do these things naturally. hell does not exist, only in the hearts of christian believers. we real humans live in Paradise…

pr

75% of info in newspapers is planted by a p.r. pro. thats why it is wise to not waste your time by reading them.   except maybe the weather, but even then, they admit to trying to control it…

dead/alive

the problem is that pharmaceuticals are keeping people alive when they should be dead. people are not honouring their date with the Mistress of Death. hence over population which leads to the world being as fucked up as it is. half the population dead = the revealing of the garden of Paradise…

valentines

st valentines. there were three different christian priests named valentine who became martyrs when they were killed for the church. ya great reason for a fucking holiday. christian dogma pretending to be real once again…

round and round

social revolution? revolution: a never ending cycle…
that just keeps going round and round and round. never actually going anywhere. hmmm…

vibration

everything has a vibration

a file?

got a package today that had a sticker on it that said that the post office had opened it for inspection… so i am trying to understand what right the government has in opening my personal mail?   i mean dont they do that in prison - check packages for a metal file and shit? am i a prisoner?

equanimous

newtons third law of motion: for every action is an equal and opposite reaction. love and hate are energetically the same thing. just different ends of the same spectrum. meditation is working on remaining equanimous. no reaction at all staying in the middle and thereby rising above them…

nibiru

nibiru did not seed life on Earth. life on Earth was etheric before the crash with nibiru. the crash itself threw us down dimensionally and this is how life started appearing in the 3rd dimension…

freaky

let your freak flag fly...

crude oil

they say a person can consume three pounds of crude oil a day: 1. your car. 2. your personal products.   3. your food (!?)

home

   home is outrageous, romantic, sharing, moonlight, exciting, dancing, dinner, friendship, making, growing, baking, tea, fun, art, music, wrestling, gardening, massaging, having baths, bunnies, hot, waterslides, nature walks, cups of steaming arguing, hammocks, gathering, standing up, crystals, cats & dogs, sunsets, making love, crying, flowers, swimming, truth, relaxing, meditating, colour, blankets, painting, exploring sound, learning, horses, cookies, a new pair of shoes, stars…
   home is free of borders, money, jobs, time, things to do, fighting, id cards, bank machines, cars, street lights, hitting, nauseous, traffic jams, grocery stores, line ups, mortgages, war, guns, suits, screaming, tazers, immigration, tv, drugs, violence, advertising, bulletins, sirens, being wasted, elevators, pain killers, straightjackets, pharmaceutical, cops, advertising, grabbing, pushing, name calling, medication, filling in forms, bars, schedules, presidents, loud noises…

priorities

1709 people died from supposed terrorism this year but 910 000 died form heart disease...

divided

so who decided long ago how the land was divided and who got to own what?

non organic

your average non-organic vegetable contains as many as 42 or more different synthetic chemicals (wtf!?)...

glory glory

i am The Scarlet Woman and i am here to bring the glory of the stars into your heart

valkyries

valkyries. the warrior death priestesses of odin. seven feet tall with golden armour. thick hair past their asses. battle axes strapped to their backs. received the souls of slain heroes with a horn of mead and lead them to the grand halls of valhalla

pyramids

we dont know how they actually built the pyramids so why did we forget? why were people smarter in the past?

emanating

as the fool emanates from the Void, the magickian emanates from the fool...

Imbolc

the first festival of spring. traditionally a time of the first milk from livestock and the first flowers of spring. a great time to cleanse and purify. perfect time to clean your house!... hint hint

spirals

the end of your fingertips are spirals...

satan

"satan" is as much of a christian lie as "god" is...

when you are lost in the darkness - focus on your central Sun! (goal)

shift

"...the Earth is approaching a time continuum shift between 2000-2017. this continuum shift represents a literal planetary time acceleration as Earths particle base accelerates in pulsation rhythm. the particle that compose the human auric field will also increase in pulsation rhythm if the physical body and bio-neurological structure of the body are not prepared to synthesize the faster pulsation particles of the auric field.

   this time acceleration will manifest as acceleration of the cellular deterioration process in order to accelerate the pulsation rhythm of the body's particles. the seed crystal seal must be release, to unlock the body particles form the pulsation rhythms of dimensions 1-3 the star crystal seals are activated by awakening the dormant morphogenetic chakra centers and drawing new frequency patterns through the chakra system into the star crystal seals activation.

   release of the crystal seals creates activation of the dormant silicate matrix dna fire codes which in turn manufactures

blood-crystal structures that raise the bodys metabolic rate and prepare the body for cellular acceleration..."
~ ashayana deane - *voyagers II - the secrets of amenti*

pan

pan, pandemonium, panic, panties, panegyric, pantomime, panther, pandemic, panacea, panache, panorama, pantheism, pant, pandanus, panoply, pang, pandour, pandowdy, pancake, pandora, pander, panchromatic, panchax, pander...

thoughts

   thoughts are chemical grooves formed in your brain. so you tend to think the same things, the same way over and over again. your energy traveling down these grooves (narrow minded?) unhealthy food and chemicals also create these thought tracks in your mind. and then there are millions of people thinking the same things you are. oh i need money oh i need love. oh i am angry. these are called thought bands. they are accumulated energy that encircle the Earth (its real). you can control your mind and you can control what you think. marijuana is one alchemical means of dissolving these chemical grooves in your mind. that is why it is illegal. because there are forces out there who dont want you to be in control of your thoughts and have a balanced brain...

black velvet triangle

   "now there is naught but a vast black triangle having the apex downwards, and in the centre of the black triangle is the face of typhon, the lord of the tempest, and he crieth aloud: despair! despair!
   for thou mayest deceive the virgin, and thou mayest cojole the mother; but what wilt thou say unto the ancient whore that is throned in eternity?
for if she will not, there is neither force nor cunning, nor any wit, that may prevail upon her.
   thou canst not woo her with love, for she *is* love. and she hath all, and hath no need of thee. and thou canst not woo her with gold, for all the kings and captains of the earth, and all the gods of heaven, have showered their gold upon her.
thus hath she all, and hath no need of thee.
   and thou canst not woo her with knowledge, for knowledge is the thing that she hath spurned. she hath it all, and hath no need of thee. and thou canst not woo her with wit, for her lord is wit.
she hath it all, and hath no need of thee. despair! despair!
   nor canst thou cling to her knees and ask for pity; nor canst thou cling to her heart and ask for love; nor canst thou put thine arms about her neck, and ask for understanding; for thou had all these, and they avail thee not. despair! despair!...
   nor canst thou win her with the sword, for her eyes are fixed upon the eyes of him in whose hand is the hilt of the sword. despair! despair!... nor canst thou win her by the serpent, for it was the serpent that seduced her first. despair! despair!"
~ aleister crowley - *the cry of the 2nd aethyr, which is called arn*

feelin it

are you numb?

Mother Earth

i love my Mother Earth

ziggurats

   human women stolen and raped by the 'sons of god.' reptilian metallic robotic Fallen Angels. stealing human women and taking them to their sex palaces on the top of ziggurats (stepped pyramids). in mesopotamia (the old iraq). usually the women didnt survive. these rapes sometimes produced anunnaki/human hybrids who became legendary demi-gods like gilgamesh, hercules, noah, enoch. hey dont think that human men were left out. they were raped by anunnaki females. these births produced eggs though because the anunnaki are reptiles...

the abuse that surrounds sexual connections with people today stems from our abusive interactions over the last hundreds of thousands of years with the anunnaki Fallen Angels...

initiation

i got sucked into the centre of the Earth and spat out somewhere in the Universe. i am a star. then i had to find my way home molecule by molecule... the same as the egyptian initiations that happened at the great pyramid...

blame eve

the church blamed women for the existence of death because eve supposedly ate the apple thereby causing death in humans. that is why priests of God are celibate, wifeless and childless. they figure if they dont have anything to do with women they will somehow be able to out dance death. silly priests...

faerieland wants you

magick, Faeries, witches, warlocks, Dragons, Fallen Angels, spells, queens & kings are all true. Faerie Tales are true! you are witch! you are wizard! you are magickian! Faerieland want you! mushrooms are your friends!

12/12/12

is the date that is the end of the mayan calendar. it is when our Sun moves fully into the photon band. it is when we move into the age of aquarius. basically we will be fully aligned with the centre of our galaxy. the synchronicities are mind-boggling. its a great time to not be ignorant about the shift dont you think?

thank Goddess

every watch, computer, radio and telephone system have a natural quartz crystal seed in them that makes them work. hey thanks Goddess - we are so dependent on you!

secret

"secret = secretions. ritu = red = ritual. secret ritual = star fire = consuming menstrual blood. Moon blood gold of the Gods - vehicle of light - primary source of manifestation - mystical waters of creation - flow of eternal wisdom - elixir rubeus - therapeutic healing - lunar essence of the Goddess - flow-er (she who flows) - nectar of supreme excellence - soma - ambrosia - blood as the vehicle of the spirit. jehovah eventually prohibits the ingestion of blood - he did not want people to be enlightened..."
~ laurence gardner

humans as slaves

"to preserve humans as a slave race and to prevent future rebellion, humans 12 strands of dna were spliced down to two strands of dna. spiritual knowledge was repressed. humans were scattered geographically into different linguistic groups and conditions were created to make physical survival on Earth an all-consuming chore from birth until death. the arrangement was to be maintained indefinitely for as long as the anunnaki Fallen Angels possessed Earth. in contrast, the modern view is that human beings had evolved accidentally from "star stuff" into slime, into fishes, into monkeys, and finally into people. the modern view actually seems more fanciful than the real one..."
~ peter r. farley - *where were you before the tree of life?*

shit nest?

when are humans going to stop shitting in their nest?

what is going on here?

psychotropic

there are psychotropic plants that have been used for millions of years by humans. these plants are our sacred ecstatic divine heritage. dmt, psilocybin, ergine, ibogaine, mescaline, peyote, san pedro, cannabis, ayahuasca, etc... these plants connect humans to the Earth because they are natural and non-synthetic. they can move you past the blockages of energy you have. so you can experience life in a very magnified, magickal and exciting way. they can help you experience the oneness of reality. placing you in the fold of the Creatrix with the plants, animals and minerals around you which can lead to an greater understanding of not wanting to harm yourself, others or the Earth and reconnect you with your soul...

Earth

every living system is in decline. meaning the 3rd dimension of Earth is dying...
do not forget there are 12 more dimensions to our Earth and ourselves!

shrinking

the catholic churchs finances are shrinking because of all the court cases against it
by the thousands and thousands of boys who were sexually abused at the hands of the church "fathers"...

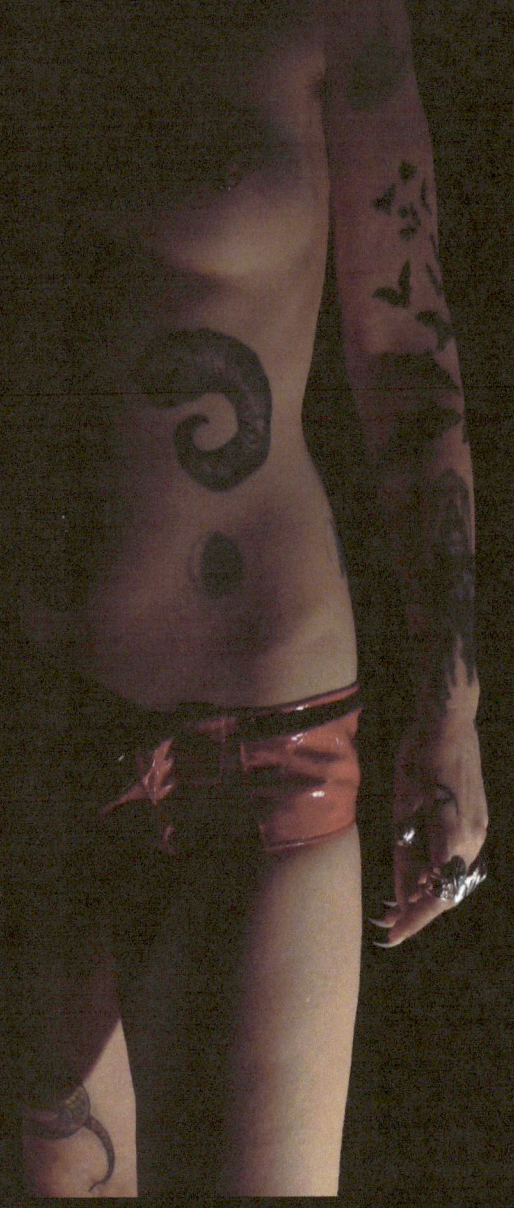

secrets of immortality

the secrets of immortality: grounding, intention, breathing, spinning, water, balance

atomic warfare

there is evidence of ancient atomic warfare in egypt, north america, india, libya, mesopotamia, sumer, peru, scotland, scandinavia and china...

stonehenge

  stonehenge. a vortex that connects you with Creatrix. authority has placed rubber mats around it to walk on. rubber will not allow energy to pass through it so you are not receiving the Goddess energy from the ground. authority has given you this little headset to listen to about the history of stonehenge. the electromagnetic energy coming off the headset interferes with the energy coming down from God. this natural vortex spins clockwise as do most vortexes created with sarsen stones. authority controls the direction people walk with little fences so they have people walking counterclockwise so you are spinning the incorrect way. thereby not receiving the energy from the vortex at all. so you have stonehenge a natural vortex but when you visit it authority has controlled your energetic experience so when you leave you have not felt a thing... when really you should have been cleansed, purified and uplifted. authority tries to control the energy of Earth and the way you interact with it. there is a war going on and its not only in the middle east...

atlantis

atlantis was the last high-technology society on Earth. technology used without heart got out of control and destroyed it. the secret government does not want you to know about atlantis because then you would realize they are exactly repeating the mistakes of the past...

hungry?

arent you hungry for more?

the great unveiling

the royalty of old are intermingling with the peasants. the blood lines are all mixed together like never before. they made it into something that will work for us in the end. never before have so many people lived at once. strip people of their money to see them for what they really are. when the great unveiling takes place we will all have such a laugh. because we all switched places for the last aeon. the peasants are queens. the kings are tinkers. the warriors are peasants.

death of the ego

i am a mirror.   i am - am i? how can you know about yourself unless others tell you? the best way of self improvement is through death of the ego. honesty without judgement. tell people exactly what you think. be honest and listen when they return the favour. learn to accept how others really are by accepting yourself - as you are.

the morrighan

"the name morrighan (mor rigan) means "great queen." she is always fully armed with a spear in each hand. the morrighan... often shape-shifts into a black crow and frequently appears as a crow on the battlefield.
　her cry is both fierce and irresistible and is said to have been as loud and formidable as the cries of ten thousand warriors. in celtic myth the cry of the Dragon is a terrifying shriek indicating waste or neglect at the hands of unworthy kings.   the Dragon is another celtic symbol of the Goddess. when the Dragon cries, it is not so much a plaintive weeping as it is a hideous scream from unbearable pain and betrayal. the morrighan possesses a similar sensitivity.   she has the ability to protect and nurture, but like the Dragon, reject her or betray her and she is impossible to soothe."
~ laurie cabot - *the witch in every woman*

mary mary quite contrary

mary magdalene really was a whore. a tantric whore. so when her and jesus got together they were actually tantric masters who taught their brethren the ways of sex magick. this is why the church tried to hide her away because then people would be having orgiastic rituals that did not include the priests (or that maybe did!)...

fraud

the donation of constantine was a fraudulent document. the document that supposedly gave the roman church the legal right to be the representatives of christ on Earth was forged. the church has no legal foundation whatsoever to hold authority on planet Earth. all institutions under their jurisdiction are illegal including european monarchy, commonwealth and all governments under their direction. all laws made under them are illegal as well...

big daddy

are you obedient to the big daddy in the sky? (sarcasm & humour)

duality

love and hate are energetically the same thing...

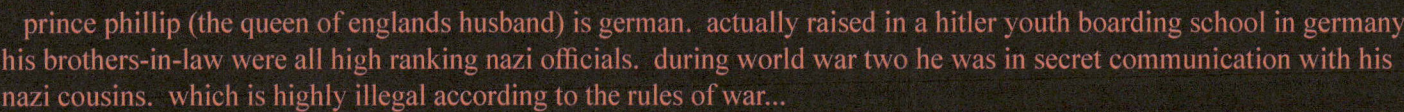

fill

  prince phillip (the queen of englands husband) is german. actually raised in a hitler youth boarding school in germany. his brothers-in-law were all high ranking nazi officials. during world war two he was in secret communication with his nazi cousins. which is highly illegal according to the rules of war...

  eventually the washington times found out and these secret communiques fell into the hands of the american army. i guess the house of windsor was desperate to keep them classified. i wonder why... think about that for a second, 60 million lives lost and the leaders of opposing side (axis and allies) are related by blood and secretly communicating? remind me again what so many people died for?

time of wonder

we truly are in a time of wonder. just as the pendulum has swung to a time of the patriarch. it once swung the other way in the time of the matriarch. but now is the time when the pendulum will not swing at all. a grace period of balance. it rests as one would in an oasis. and magick will once again become one with the land. male and female united two as one. balance between Goddess and God - represented by Creatrix…

thirteenth school

"…according to the lemurian fellowship…the elders of lemuria, known as the "thirteenth school," moved their headquarters prior to the [pole-shift] cataclysm to the uninhabited plateau of central asia that we now call tibet. here they supposedly established a library and a mystery school, and became known as "the great white brotherhood..."
~ david hatcher childress

helectites

helectites are spiral stalactites that defy gravity because they grow sideways, not down
showing how molecules can exist outside of space and time

survival of the fittest

survival of the fittest keeps humanity strong. fuck pharmaceutical drugs. fuck welfare. fuck charity. fuck saving people. they only weaken the human genome

Curse of the Crone

  old women were considered the closest to the Goddess. because they no longer bled ,they were thought to be the one most in balance. their judgment was always trusted - following the Laws of Nature. they would lay the "Curse of the Crone" on those who were condemned to die. if their behaviour was not to the benefit of the whole. this was how the balance of life was kept intact. the power of life and death was then taken from the old women.

  and now we have pharmaceutical drugs and jail. because of this the balance of nature is completely fucked up. authority was taken and placed into the hands of a system instead of the people governing themselves. we must reclaim our ability to govern ourselves instead of letting the system of authority make the rules of life for us humans

psychic dictatorship

this psychic dictatorship breeds a psychotic reality in which the sane person is a minute percentage...

normal is alien

shame because we are not "normal." there is no such thing as "normal." "normal" is alien.

God and fallen Angels

its so much easier to think of God as something far and so much less personal
instead of knowing about Fallen Angels which are very close and very personal...

war on consciousness

isnt facebook a perfect example of the war on consciousness? monitored, controlled and forced to comply...

freedom

can you imagine a world with no police? yes! yes i can!

common sense hint

take care of your teeth. rotten teeth makes you really cranky.
they are very poisonous. go to the dentist regularly.

emotions

be wary of spiritual practices with others or leaders that want you to intentionally express emotions.

Ostara

happy Spring Equinox or ostara named after a Goddess of spring, fertility, rebirth, and the rising Sun. one of the Sabbats of the Wheel of the Year where day and night are equal. festival of new growth, renewal, a re-balancing of energies and the return of longer days...

faeries

   "so, you see, 'Fairies' are not something twee and biddable; once they were giants, and they can be warriors, fierce and frightening, who know the light and shade and taste of the soul. you may also consider them mercenaries, fighting for their purpose, which is freedom and the return to their original form so that they, too, can evolve beyond their enchantment. what they will never do is acquiesce to your bidding like some genie from a bottle. but if you make them your friends, you will find no stronger or more loyal allies. this is why i call them 'Angels' and their tempestuous nature is why i refer to them as creatures of storms. they are the natural energies of the Earth. they help us our healing work and can summon the air and the elements to blow through us, carrying away illness and illusion as if a gale was howling in our souls the way to meet them for the first time is at night, and we must prepare for our encounter thoroughly..."
~ ross haven - *the sin eater's last confessions*

astral traveling

good way to learn about how to move your spirit, as in astral traveling. learning to travel within and without. take your focus/I AM presence/attention/consciousness and bring it within and sit. then take it and put it without on your mouth or nose for example. communicating is without. within is heart. within is breathe. you can learn to feel the difference.

zip

zipper method people! that means i have a turn, you have a turn. i have a turn, you have a turn... go with flow.

licking good time

licking your plate is a compliment to the chef.

magick work

your level of magick is a perfect reflection of the work you do.
it is an eye for an eye kind of relationship...

udjat eye

udjat

udjat eye represents the three levels of consciousness:
the snake on the ground - the human eye on the Earth - the vulture in the air...

awareness

bringing awareness to something is enough to shift it...

Earth Angel

she is alive and can hear you. tell her your name.
the Goddess wants to hold you in this upcoming change...

system suckers

the system traps you in its tedium and then it sucks you dry... it is designed to work at the pace of an earthworm to drive you crazy! the matrix is true. you are stuck in a consciousness devouring net. the more you give ~ the more it takes. the lines, the slow traffic, the street lights, the bureaucracy, the paperwork, the rules, the waiting, the conformity. oh the red tape of it all! when humans are stressed they are easily controlled and they give off stress pheromones. can you imagine there is a powerful fucker at the very top profiting from it all? he is a 4th dimensional archetype who eats, consumes and glories in your stress... the world is specifically designed to be exactly this way! eat the fucking red pill already!

God time

the Dark Goddess is kali time, Goddess time or Creatrix time...

vampyre

creating psychodrama (ie conflict) because others are not conforming to your expectations
is the play of the energetic vampyre...

hungry

stores at the holiday seasons are like hungry sparkly vaginas. "come in me" they plead...

piezoelectric

dna and quartz are piezoelectric. they produce electricity or charge under pressure. they are like a slinky.   as the long wave (sound) increases, the short wave (voltage) decreases because they are mechanically connected...
~ dan winter

coincidences

coincidences are the realm of the Dark Goddess. she is sending them to you for a reason…

burning

it takes roughly twenty minutes to go unconscious
when you are being burned at the stake...

they say

they say that when lsd flooded the world in 1969. it raised the vibration of society and finally allowed the light of consciousness to flood the Earth plane. therefore star children were able to be born. those born after 1969 are different...
~ drunvalo melchizedek - *the ancient secret of the flower of life*

apocalypse

when the apocalypse comes you will go to where you believe you are going. you do not have to panic. be in your heart. be connected to Mother Earth. be with people you love, doing what you love. focus on your goals. be yourself.

memoire of a death priestess

memoir of a death priestess: flew into new york city today. had planned to have lunch in this nice organic cafe. get there and have to pry my way through the crowd. i guess a lady had jumped just a few minutes before. i continued on with my lunch but out of the corner of my eye can see this white shrouded corpse just ten feet away. the energy was intense. the crowd of people were mental, taking pictures! not to mention the soup i was eating was the saltiest thing ever. coincidence? death with lunch or lunch with death anyone?...

quirky

when the russians defeated berlin in 1945 they found over 1000 tibetan monks who had committed ritual suicide while wearing nazi officer uniforms...

birds

at the end of the day, just before bed, watching birds on youtube with my little kitty stella...

antenna

believer/unbeliever. the foundation for magick is belief. if you dont have it - you wont see it. there is no proof except for that which resides in your heart, your feelings, your senses and your antenna...

ego-fucking

judging others is a reflection of your own self hate. it is a waste of time because your energy is placed outside instead of inside. it does not further your own spiritual evolution and therefore is ego-fucking...

sauntering

sauntering through the woods in the wee hours of the morning on a spring night!...

day what

my cats do not understand why daylight savings has to affect their dinnertime...

maximum bliss potential

for maximum bliss potential - your internal and external realities should be the same...

odds

apocalypse. the Earths natural cleansing cycle. everything synthetic will vibrate itself into destruction. so if there is synthetic shit in your blood and veins, it will kill you...

sex strike

women in liberia had a sex strike to force their men to stop the war that was ripping their country apart (it worked)...

new green of spring

"the new green of spring following the resurrection of horus. the new doctrine of the tetragrammaton, where the earthly component, he final, the daughter, is set upon the throne of the mother, to awaken the eld of the all-father..."

~ aleister crowley - *the book of thoth*

neva
you can never go back...

adds up
its the little things...

its all about vibration and it is a choice

now
repair energy field now.

arrow
your will is an arrow...

animal
when you eat an animal you are allowing that animal to experience your vibration so he knows there is another level of existence. thereby aiding him on his reincarnational path towards becoming a human

shadow tripping
we all have a shadow of ignorance that trails along behind us.
sometimes it sneaks its way round to trip us up...

leaping lizards
"the goat leaping with lust upon the summits of the Earth..."
~ aleister crowley - *the book of thoth*

explain this!
here is a list of things that have been found in the world that defy modern scientific timelines

so how do you explain? :
*copper coin discovered in illinois, found in rock deposits that are 200 000 to 400 000 years old
*modern human skeleton discovered in tanzania, cemented in rock deposits dated as 800 000 years old
*modern human skull discovered in buenos aires, found in rock deposit dated 1 to 1.5 million years old
*small human carved figurine discovered in idaho, found in layers of clay dated from 2 million years old
*modern human skull discovered in italy, found in rock deposits dated from 3 to 4 million years old
*sea shell carved with a human face found in england, found in stratified rock deposits dated 2 to 2.5 million years old
*ball discovered in france, found in rock deposits dated 45 to 55 million years old
*mortar and pestle discovered in california, found in gravel deposits dated 55 million years old
*metallic tube discovered in france, found embedded in a chalk bed dating over 65 million years old
*shoe sole fossilized in rock discovered in nevada, found in rock dated from 213 to 248 million years ago
*gold thread discovered in england, found in rock deposit dated from 320 to 360 million years old
*linked gold chain discovered in illinois, found embedded in coal dated from 260 to 320 million years old
*iron pot discovered in oklahoma, found in coal dated from 600 million years old
*grooved metal spheres (hundreds discovered) in africa, found embedded in sediment dated from 2.8 billion years old
~ forbidden knowledge - bibliotecapleyades

murder

love watching my local murder of crows dropping nuts from up high to crack them open and swooping down to eat them...

abandonment

"abandonment to desire introduces the seeds of decay into the fruit of pleasure..."
~ aleister crowley - *the book of thoth*

dreams

dreams really do come true. if you focus upon them enough...

validity

arguing with others over details is the sign of insecurity. why are people not allowed to express their opinions without being attacked for every nuance of what they are saying by the over-active left-brains of others? we all see and value things differently. it seems that those who like to correct need their egos stoked and to somehow collect the power of being "right." why can we not share what we know in a loving and safe environment? knowledge comes from both the rational and the irrational parts of the mind. and in the end all opinions are valid, whether they are "right" or not...

farsight

the farsight of priestesses was traditionally consulted to predict the outcome of worldly affairs because it was always considered far more accurate than the reasoning of men...

angles

you can study something for 30 years...
but if you are not holding your head at the right angle you wont learn a thing...

equal

spirit and matter are equal, yet opposite expressions of the same thing. one is not greater or less important than the other...

at all

didnt your mother tell you if you dont have anything nice to say
then dont say anything at all?...

ah

the gods of war can go fuck themselves...

fallen Angels

the Fallen Angels live in the 4th dimension
thats the realm of the imagination
they use fear-based media to arouse your emotions
where do your emotions go once activated?
the hungry mouth of the Fallen Angel as he sucks
your vital life essence from your pineal gland!

the veils

the veils are thinning and will continue to do so until they disappear. what this means is that entities from other
dimensions are leaning on our Earth (3rd dimensional) boundaries. simply put... they are looking for hosts.
as the veils thin, we will see more and more than does not rightfully belong here...

she is so vast

speaking of the Dark Goddess: "she is the Creatrix of the Universe, older than time, vaster than space. she is the cause
and mother of the world, the one primordial being. she is pure being-consciousness-bliss, the power existing in the form

of time and space, and everything they contain, the radiant illuminatrix in all beings.

she is the great cause, the primordial energy, the great effulgence, more subtle than the subtlest elements. the gods themselves said to her, "thou art the original of all manifestations; thou art the birthplace of even us; thou knowest the whole world, yet none know thee...

thou art the beginning of all, Creatrix, protectress, and destructress. all gods are born of her body, and at the time of dissolution (doomsday) they would again disappear into her. she is the material cause of all change, manifestation and destruction. the whole world rests upon her, rises out of her and melts away into her.

from her are crystallized the original elements and qualities which construct the apparent worlds. she is both matter and grave. she is so vast that the series of Universes appear and disappear with the opening and shutting of her eyes..."
~ barbara g walker – *the crone*

clash

i do not believe in evil/good. but i do know the clash between ego/spirit and the difference between tension/relaxation

eventually

eventually the slave will become the master...

order

light is order. neutrality is neutral. dark is chaos. light is uncaring because it is just shining. neutral is neutral. it is the dark that cares because it is the one that keeps the balance...

aliens in bible

the book of enoch (noahs grandfather) spoke of aliens: "...a whirlwind carried me off from the Earth... i saw a great and glorious device... i looked and saw a lofty throne: its appearance was as crystal and the wheels thereof as the shining Sun... from underneath the throne came streams of flaming fire so great that i could not look thereon.... and i saw in the heaven running in the world, above those portals in which revolve the stars that never set... ...portals of the heaven open. and i saw how the stars of heaven come forth..."

diamond

it takes the deepest darkest Earth to make the brightest light of the diamond...

best interest at heart

women will always have the best interest of the whole at heart.
we have babies to protect! the human race would not survive otherwise...

a seed

i am the seed of the apocalypse...

witch

witches you are. the current of witches flows. what is a witch? a witch is a human. witches are real humans that believe in freedom from authority. they realize that they are the Goddess or God of their own reality. the power of the witch ebbs and flows with the Moon. the power of the government is reliant on someone flicking a switch witches walk the night with power curling at their heels. they can see deeply. they share what they know...

free of war

   there used to never be war on Earth. a reptilian humanoid Fallen Angel landed on Earth a long time ago looking for gold. gold is how they remain semi-immortal and how they try to replicate the power of their souls. Earth is the largest source of gold in the Universe. one an Angel. one a Fallen Angel. so these brothers who have different mothers come to Earth and with them bring this concept of war. basically it is sibling rivalry for the throne on their home planet. they got tired of mining for gold though and so being master geneticists starting fucking with the local humans to turn them into slaves for the gold mines.
   they took our 12 strands of dna and spliced it down to two strands of dna and totally interfered with our divine heritage. we are the Guardians of Earth - and Earth is the heart chakra of the Universe. these brothers seeded their own conflict into our blood. and hence the history of nuclear war, murder, kingship and the bullshit patriarchal control has resulted.
   so you see war never used to be on Earth - and when we reach critical mass of knowing this information, we will be able to collectively let our hearts shine, which in turn can make the Earths heart shine and we will exorcise these Fallen Angels parasitic motherfuckers from our home and rightfully take our places as the Guardians of Earth once again...

celts held rome siege

i remember when romans had to pay us celts wagons full of gold. so we would stop holding rome under siege...

aeons

old aeon = negative outdated masculine out of balance bullshit from the past...

human

i dont care what gods or goddesses you believe in. you are still a human...

try harder

i would rather know you will try harder next time than to hear you say sorry...

appearances

the world only appears to be shitty right now
because we are cleaning out our collective dark psychic content
just do not attach to things as they move through you...

elders of nope

the protocols of the elders of zion (in other words the plans for new world order by the illuminati): *right is might. *poverty is our weapon. *masses led by lies. *universal war. *we name presidents. *free press destroyed. *only lies printed. *secret societies. *we demand submission. *we shall be cruel. *we shall rewrite history. *govern with fear. *destroy capital. *cause financial depression. *instilling obedience and the list goes on...

star warrior

ten commandments of the star warrior
1. i am a child of the dancing star born of chaos. 2. i am fire. 3. i see the fire in all things. 4. i am but a visitor in the land

of living things. 5. i walk the path of silence. 6. i am not seen or heard, i am only felt. 7. i take only that which i can return. 8. i cannot possess, i can only share. 9. i am great spirit in all ways. 10. i am the answer...
~ robert morning sky

actively

if you are not actively working at improving yourself you are sliding down a slippery slope...

outside

i am the Angel of Death. Firstborn. i come from corrections: Sacred Law. i am an agent of the 13th dimension, the Void. outside of this dimensional reality. outside. i am a death priestess. i am an exorcist. i am a grim reaper...

baalbek lebanon

in lebanon there is a colossal platform carved out of perfectly shaped blocks of stone weighing 600, 900 and 1000 tons each (the stones of the pyramid weigh only 200 tons each). a few miles away in the quarry where the stones came from is a stone half quarried... it weighs over 1200 tons and is perfectly straight (which is near impossible to do). there is no machinery or crane on the planet that can lift a 1200 ton stone today... but the Fallen Angels who were using them for their spaceship landing pad sure could...

sacred behaviour

words taken and perverted by authority figures like psychiatrists who label and condemn those who do not conform to what scientists believe to be the truth. lunatic. luna = Moon. lunatic = Moon worshiper. a lunatic is a witch that dances naked under a full Moon. a perfect example of how sacred behaviour is made to appear to be a sickness and profane.

necrophagous sorceress

the necrophagous sorceress dwells in every Moon worshiper. she lives in the shadow of the Moon and punishes sins of violence against the Mother. she is the deadly mistress of nightmares, phantoms and madness...

creating

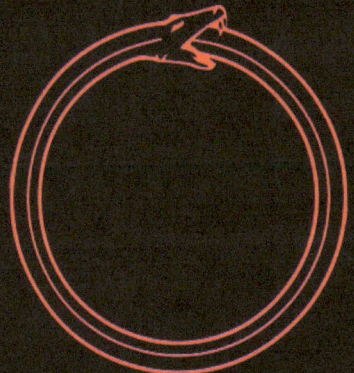

your consciousness creates your body...

atoms are galaxies

to a flea our atoms are galaxies...

mistress or slave

reincarnation is very real. you are either a Firstborn, a Onceborn, or somewhere in between. so the nazis may kill the jews. but then they are born a jew and have to suffer what they created. or your a chinese soldier killing a tibetian monk and then you get born a monk. that is going to get killed by a chinese soldier. what goes around comes around the slave is really the mistress. the mistress is really the slave...

severe

you think i am severe? you should meet my mistress, the Dark Goddess...

acceptance

it is wise to accept the love the Universe is sending your way...

you are

deaths desire...

cenzor

censorship sucks ass...

before christianity

before christianity, the tribal system was based upon the leadership of elders in conjunction with the power of the shaman, medicine person or magick person of the tribe (man or woman) who would work with the wisdom of the spirits of the ancestors in relation to the land upon which they lived. the people lived in harmony and in balance with the Earth asking permission to take only what they needed and being grateful for whatever they received. the tribal system is billions of years old.

   then the christian missionaries traveled to most of the countries in the world. blackrobes or Otherwise magicians as they were called. with them they brought smallpox and bibles so the tribal people were either killed with disease. (95% of the population) or forcibly made to convert to christianity. you were killed if you did not convert. the children were separated from their parents and put into residential schools.

   where they were not allowed to speak their native tongue, see their parents or families, forced to go to church, forced to study the bible and were beaten by the nuns if they failed to comply.

   in this process the history, spirituality and ways of the tribal people were eradicated. their sacred places and practices were torn asunder. the sacred forests were burnt. the ancestral graves were desecrated. the native oral traditions were disrupted with alcohol and were replaced with war, torture, disease and famine.

   this happened all over the world and with all of the different races. the church burnt millions of women, gay people and 'heretics' at the stake. basically anyone who disagreed with their doctrine of control. and in the process took all of the land, animals, gold, jewels, sacred treasures of the tribal peoples of the world. the church burnt all of the history and then wrote their own. they created a false doctrine that keeps the human race in control, in fear and subservient to authority. instead in harmony and in balance with the Earth.   it is now a long time past since these atrocities happened so long the memories of the tribal people has been so raped and plundered. that the people themselves dont really remember what happened and just believe what the winners have written. but there are some of us who do remember the truth and the truth always prevails.

   heres a list of countries that were decimated of their original tribes, ancestors, history, culture and ways of being i found in just five minutes of research... witches, knights templar, england, ireland, scotland, japan, east indies, australia, oceana, gays, south africa, central africa, northwest africa, northeast africa, the european crusades, jews in europe, african islands, south america, blacks in america, angola, central, america, the pacific islands, hawaii, caribbean islands, north america, mexico, philippines, burma, thailand, vietnam, china, india…

apocalypse

apocalypse. your imagination will become real as we ascend back to the 5th dimension. its a good idea to work through your fears now. so when the shift comes you will not be scared to death by your own dark psychic content...

nuit says

nuit says that "the key to the rituals is in the secret word which i have given unto him (the priest Beast)."   this revealing of the Beast and The Scarlet Woman will be made at a certain moment when the time is right.
i wonder, does the word burn on your lips?...

toxic

toxic individuals in control of occult information = sorcery...

war sucks

there were no weapons of mass destruction and your government sent in your military and murdered hundreds of thousands of innocent men, women, children of iraq... now your country is laden with anti-terrorism laws that completely violate your personal freedoms. what are you doing about it? there is a great movie about this called the end of america...

the card game

Fallen Angels rule the land. and we play right into their hand. whose to say there is right or wrong. we should have followed are hearts all along. the deck is cut. the cards are drawn. its time to stop being a pawn!

ley lines

ley lines are the magnetic energy lines that circle the Earth. now, on every ley line crossing is a church, military station, government building or police station because they harvest the energy of the Dragon pathways.
your government knows magick - do you?...

the Wheel of the Year

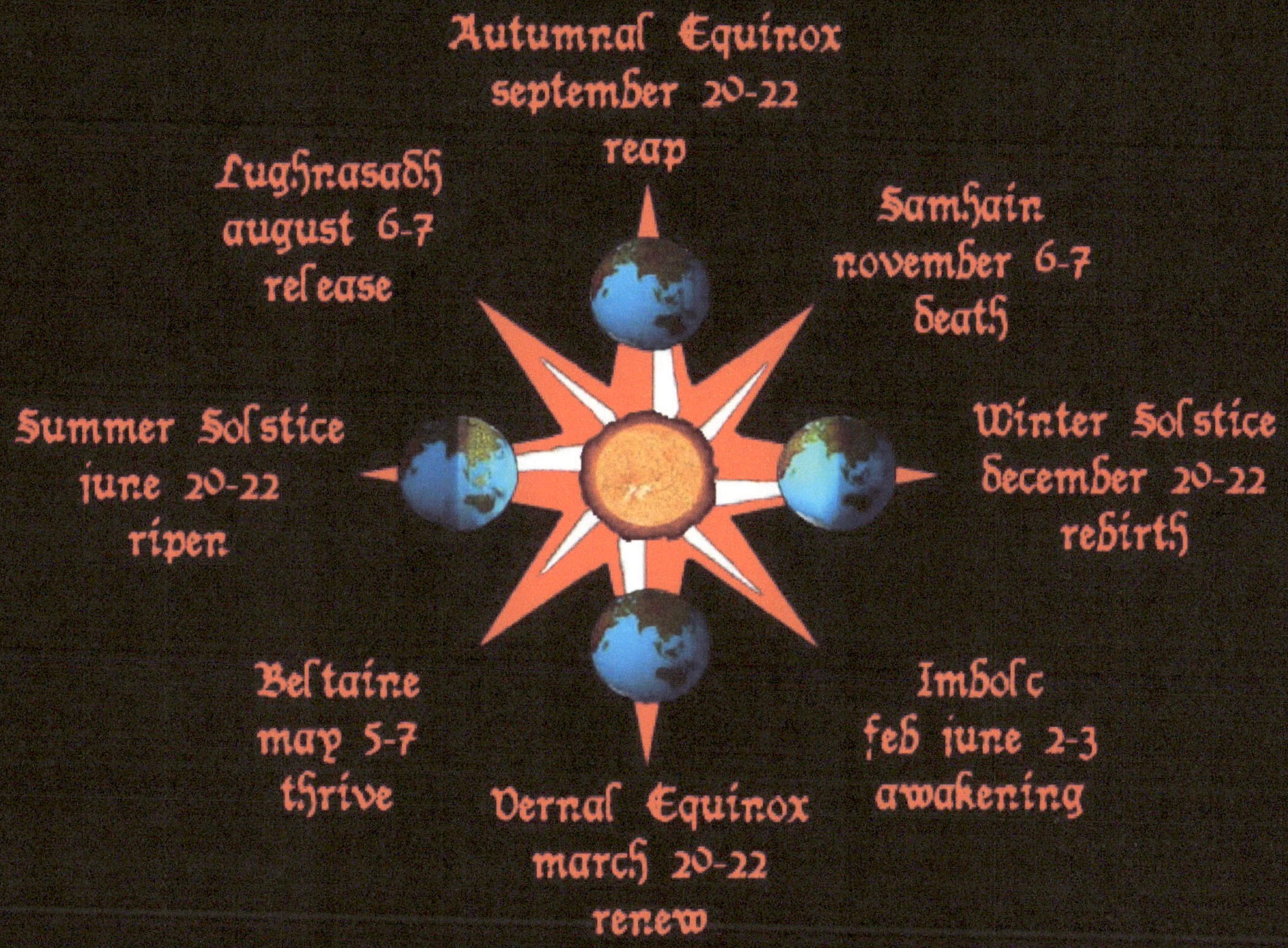

Autumnal Equinox
september 20-22
reap

Lughnasadh
august 6-7
release

Samhain
november 6-7
death

Summer Solstice
june 20-22
ripen

Winter Solstice
december 20-22
rebirth

Beltaine
may 5-7
thrive

Imbolc
feb june 2-3
awakening

Vernal Equinox
march 20-22
renew

survival mode

   society is pumped with so much fear (violence, media, police, rules, war, etc.). a human body reacts to fear by going into survival mode. the body craves food with really high fat levels and really high sugar levels when it is in survival mode. no wonder people are fat... and since corporations, militaries and governments are all owned by a really small elite group of rich old men - i wonder if they are doing that on purpose? (sarcasm). when the human is in survival mode they tend to go a little manic and do things they wouldnt normally do like spend money on needless things, party more, are nervous and will tend to sway with the pack mentality more. they will simply be more controllable...

gratitude

gratitude is everything

soul blood

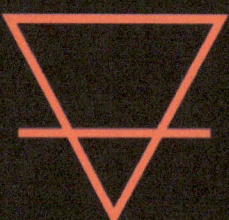

blood. the war on consciousness is taking place in your blood. your soul resides in your blood. you carry the information you learn through your reincarnational cycles in your blood. so if the Otherwise brotherhood can convince you to contaminate your blood this totally effects your access to your soul. therefore you have a bunch of soulless motherfuckers walking the land. the soulless are easily possessed by the Otherwise. the purer your blood of contaminants the more your soul resides in your body. the more soul you have - the brighter you shine. the more people who shine - the less the Otherwise can feast of the souls of the innocent. the war on consciousness is taking place in your blood...

just dont do it

you do not have to take others peoples shit on... (permission granted to let it all go!)

bliss

organic forms of bliss are the only way to save yourself...

eternal moment

have you noticed that time is speeding up? time is collapsing in on itself. before there were only so many moments in a second and now because of technology and computers there is so much information being held in nanoseconds that each moment has become expanded eventually time will cease.   a second will become an eternity because of how much information we will be able to hold in it a moment...

confess

during the inquisition when the church burned women at the stake for being witches, they would torture you first to get a confession. i remember being repeatedly raped and they would stick these horrible metal instruments up my ass.
then they would take me to the confession room and ask me to confess to celebrating black mass orgies with satan...
i would say ~ isnt that what just happened in the other room? are you crazy motherfuckers talking about yourselves?

coming changes

"it would seem that the immediate goal of the Otherwise brothers is to delay the manifestation of the new aeon, the birth of the magical child and the realization of the ubermensch through diversion of the will-current into less than useless power plays, demoralizing materialist and superstitious delusions, new age jargon, etc..."
~ allen h greenfield - *secret cipher of the ufonauts*

roman

isnt it funny how our whole society is roman? money, politics, religion, calendar, architecture, military are all based on roman ideals. even blond anorexic girls are a dream of rome. when the romans conquered britain they ripped down all of the sacred trees and destroyed the springs. they killed all the druid priests that did not convert and raped the last of the priestesses who had not already been murdered. these priestesses had those children. they were raised and formed a secret group called the Fellowship of the Raven. those children made a pact to come back after 2000 years to avenge the murder of magick. well it has been 2000 years and the Fellowship is reforming in order to fulfill its pact. a call has been sounded to those who remember their past lives and remember the slaughter of our way of life. to reinstate magick in its rightful place of leadership across the land. the aeon of the dying god is over. the aeon of the child has come...

philadelphia experiment

philadelphia experiment
in 1943 u.s. navy tried to make a ship invisible by placing a synthetic mer-ka-ba around it. the experiment went horribly

wrong and ripped a hole in the time and space. when the ship came back from its brief time away most of the crew was injured, dying or just plain gone. men were stuck half in and half out of metal walls, some turned into puddles, some came back with limbs in the wrong place. it also ripped a dimensional hole in the time and space continuum
this is one way off-planet entities can penetrate our dimension

stand up for your freedom

they are psychiatrically screening little kids at school. if they are not normal they put them on pharmaceutical drugs (what the fuck is normal anyway?) if the parents protest they can be arrested and jailed...
what if one of those little kids is a future martin luther king, john lennon, or ghandi?

slander

the church has always used propaganda to slander their enemies. creating stories that gullible peasants still believe today. stories like witches used to steal and eat babies. and priestesses are really prostitutes. and women are bad luck...

nope

the word satan or lucifer was never in the old testament...

venus

the constant lightning activity on venus
makes her known as the electric dragon...

450

homosexuality is found in over 450 species of animals...

eye for an eye

those scientists that torture and test harsh chemicals on animals with no remorse. an elephant is known to extract revenge on someone who abused them in the past...

rainbow warrior

are you a rainbow warrior?

hint hint

people can smell your breath in small spaces...

sparkle

sparkle is the hottest currency on Earth...

Earth

Earth is a free will zone...

snowflake

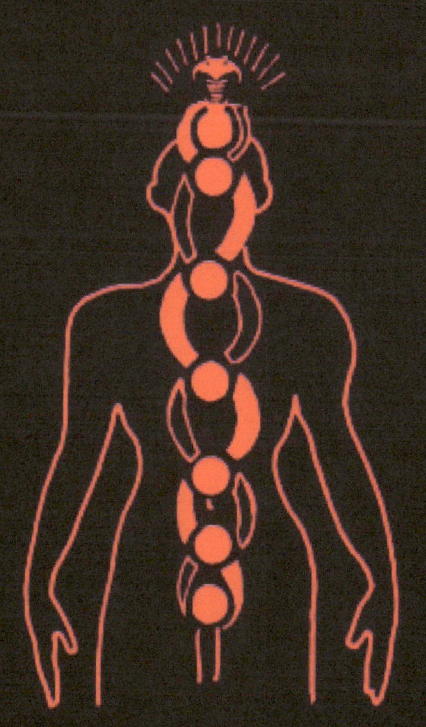

at the moment of birth your soul rockets down from the Void and penetrates your body. it takes an elevator down through the planets, space and the stars. the blueprint and the signature of your soul is created by the location of the planets in our solar system (your astrological chart) at the exact moment when your soul and body meet and then it is recorded in you. you are a snowflake...

alchemical wedding

the marriage of your male and female selves, spirit and soul, sulfur and salt, Sun and Moon, and king and queen...

Demons

we are all possessed by Demons. we are all Angels (in different stages of remembering)...

it is wise to hunt your freedom

on the gates of the nazi concentration camps
they had the words
'work shall set you free'
the only difference today
is you cant see the gates...

blood brothers

obama is bush's 11th cousin...

stick in the slavery machine

on the gates of concentration camps they had the words "work shall set you free." that is exactly like the world today. but work will never set you free - work is slavery. mostly you are working to make your boss or corporation richer. to pay the rent and so you can go out on a saturday night... the world is a huge machine comprised of a bunch of slaves working. as humans our divine right is to be imploding rainbows (?) way more than mere slaves. you could explore your personal power and find a different way to support yourself than just working for some boss...

lemurian seed crystals

lemurian seed crystal. the original barcode. they are known to hold your akashic records. your akashic records contain the information of all of your past lives, and all of the lessons you have learned. the akashic records are held at the magnetic core of the Earth. these are all the records of all beings that have ever lived on the planet. the akashic records are a good example of the collective unconscious of humans, the unlimited realm in which all of us are connected...

hmmm...

most makeup and gasoline derive from the same source...

fatty

all of the toxins you consume get stored in your fat...

initiation?

INITIATRIX

deather

you cannot live, nor can you be free, until you have died. this has nothing to do with physical death…
spiritual death. do it on purpose. dig a grave, throw a blanket on top and spend the night for example...

dark learning

i feel the pain of Mother Earth as she is being raped by heartless Fallen Angel motherfuckers. they exploit her resources by torturing her animals, mining her elements, slaughtering her plants. turning humans into zombies by controlling them feeding them with plastic and taking away their free will. funny the only way we seem to learn is with pain of the Otherwise side...

tampons

   non-organic tampons cause cancer because of synthetic chemicals. the bleach and the pesticides used on the cotton. they are a major source of ocean pollution. get a keeper Moon cup! it holds your blood and then you can dispose of your blood unto the Earth. which is the way it is suppose to be... Mother Earth loves you and loves to connect with your dna via your blood. this is how she registers who you are.
   hey guys dont feel left out Mother Earth loves your semen. blood and semen are the highest vibrational magick that humans possess. it is how the Earth keeps in touch with the humans via our dna. when you offer her your dna then she protects you and keeps you grounded. (which means your spirit stays in your body). because if you are not in your body. -who or what is? (not in body = possession by low vibrational parasitic energies, negative thoughtforms or Demons...)

mission

i have come to hell to collect you and take you back home. our mission is almost complete...

corporate programming

happy "i need a corporation to tell me how to spread my feelings" day...

"aleister crowley, speaking for the Beast 666, declares that "aiwaz solar-phallic-hermetic lucifer is his (i.e the Beasts) own Holy Guardian Angel , and the devil, satan or Hadit, of our particular unit of the starry Universe. this serpent, an, is not the enemy of man, but he who made gods of our race, knowing good and evil;

he bade know thyself and taught initiation. he is the devil of the book of thoth (the tarot card) and his emblem is baphomet, the androgyne who is hieroglyph of arcane perfection. the number of his atu (tarot, key) is xv (15), which is yod he, the monogram of the eternal, the father one which the mother, the virgin seed one with all-containing space. he is therefore life, and love.

but moreover his letter is ayin, the eye: he is light, and his zodiacal image is capricornus, that leaping goat whose attribute is liberty."
~ kenneth grant – *the magical revival*

swim in the chaos

the old aeon has ended. we are children of a new aeon. all the old rules do not apply. the old authority cannot contain us you are the Goddess or God of your fate now. learn from the old masters and then let them go. learn to swim in the chaos

angles vs curves

"beware the shadow masters and the hounds that guard the barrier.
they only travel in angles. only do souls travel in curves"
~ thoth – *emerald tablets*

courage

it takes courage to stay focused on your intended balanced outcome…

age of destruction

doctors destroy health. lawyers destroy justice. universities destroy knowledge. government destroys freedom. major media destroys information. religion destroys spirituality. dogma destroys freedom of thought…

banned

dan winter is a controversial metaphysical teacher and author. type dan winter into google. his site will not come up. it has been taken over by people claiming that he has infringed on their copyrighted material (simply untrue). they than go one a bit of a rampage saying why his work is false.
not only that but most likely your internet browser will not let you actually get to his real site (www.goldenmean.info) because somehow google has blocked him from coming up in a search. not only that if you look at the bottom of the page it tells you his work has been omitted because he is a 'fugitive' and there is a reward if you snitch on him. where the fuck is the freedom of speech in this? where is the integrity?
it is a sad day when your search engine is based on censorship…

boo emf

emf. electro magnetic frequency. radiowaves, microwaves, electrowaves, magnetic waves, power lines, home wiring, airport and military radar, substations, transformers, computers and appliances. unnatural. causes the bodys immune system to be depleted. causes way high risks of cancer, brain tumours, leukemia, birth defects, miscarriages, chronic fatigue, headaches, cataracts, heart problems, stress, nausea, chest pain, forgetfulness… (to name just a few)
not only that but those waves can be controlled from the source and can control, pervert and manipulate the thoughts of

humans. waves = mind control. we are the mice in a really fucked experiment...

be-head

in the old days they would behead you if you refused to be baptized...

yay spring

happy Spring Equinox. when night & day and light & shadow are in balance...

Demons are angry faeries

recipe for magickian

1 human. 1/4 piece fire (heart). 1/4 piece air (mind). 1/4 piece earth (body). 1/4 piece water (feelings). 1 part personal secret alchemical formula. 1 soul = magickian

dying to party

the war of the imagination is upon us. it is an alchemical war. our brains are being controlled through the alchemy we consume. alchemy gets imprinted from whence it has come. it imprints where it was made, where you get it from and your trip is affected. lsd, mushrooms, weed, e, tobacco. you are picking up on others people energy, good or bad.

if we talk about cocaine and heroin. these drugs are made through negative means. the countries they are coming from are really fucked up. the people live in serious fear, poverty, violence and under serious control. because these drugs have been exposed to the energies of war, slavery and murder. that is what you are consuming. intimately ingesting...

there is war in the world. innocent woman and children are being killed. so you can party. addiction is not cool. it makes you into a selfish unemotional robot who is really easily controlled. and you are completely supporting the war in the world and are probably totally ignorant and uncaring of that fact. where is your true will? do you even know?...

there is a difference between worshiping at night, being a nightwalker, loving the Dark. and being an uncaring motherfucker who murders someone because of a bad drug deal. there is a huge difference between the Dark side and Otherwise. there is a huge difference between focusing on spiritual evolution and reveling in personal satisfaction...

messiah

messiah: one who has been anointed with the fat of the reptile (crocodile)
so jesus was initiated into a bloodline of egyptian reptilian priests created to lead humanity...

days of olde

in the days of old we used to fight woman and man side by side. we were the Sun and Earth. working together to create the rainbow between us. there were no words, just thoughts like colours whispered back and forth like the tides. we danced and swung and pivoted together, our breaths intertwined. like the black and the white snakes that coil down and up our spines…

free of fear

there is nothing to be afraid of...

the witching hour

its the witching hour. the time to gather under the spring waxing Moon. grab your broom and ride.
where lies the Holy Sacred Regalia of the Goddess? i can hear them giggling. as the time draws near.
the reuniting of the Holy Grail with the Arc of the Covenant

every

everything is real...

neuro what

perfume and cologne are neurotoxins...

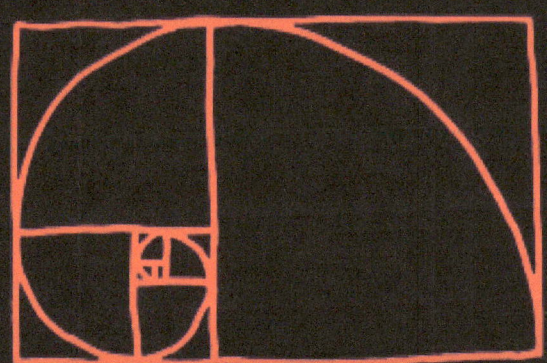

repeat

you cannot do the same things and expect change to happen...

renegade

"renegade member of family of light -- systems buster -- available for altering systems of consciousness within the free-will Universe -- on call..."
~ barbara marciniak - *bringers of the dawn*

poking pot

obsessive smoking pot is the collective heart break...

l'emotions

grief, anxiety, fear are now being classified as mental disorders instead of normal human emotions. medicate so you are a happy fucking robot... Fallen Angels do not have feelings. of course they are going to think you are crazy to have them!...

possession sucks

when you are addicted to drugs or alcohol it pushes your spirit out of your body. the synthetic chemicals in your blood do not create a hospitable environment for spirit... when your spirit is pushed out of your body it creates room for other things of a dubious nature to enter. this is how one becomes possessed by Demons.

Demons are low level energetic entities that feed off of low level energies such as anger, hatred, jealousy, violence... just go downtown on a saturday night around four am and you can see these Demons in action...

annihilation

that was the biggest mistake of the christians was to annihilate the tribes
regrouping is painful but karma is way more painful...

aha

when you say you are going to do something, your soul eagerly awaits you to honour your word, thereby increasing your ensoulment. when you do not do what you say you are going to do, your soul gets bummed, and it decreases your ability to ensoul yourself...

mental

mental concentration on symbol induces deep auto-hypnosis which releases the astral body...

control

your reality is controlled by something you cannot see, taste or touch... you can choose to live your little la-fucking-la-la life or you can dig deep, get educated and do something about it...

together

shift. the coming together of the most powerful priestess and the most powerful magickian in the land...

pain

christian martyrdom is pain and suffering. because of their god. sacrifice is not cool, it is weakness

tools

tools are training wheels...

photons

your dna absorbs and emits photons. photons which are particles of energy that burn at 5000 degrees and are a tiny piece of the Sun. meaning your dna has an intense relationship with light. your body, your etheric body, your emotions are also made up of light. meaning that your will, thoughts and your consciousness can change the state of your dna. meaning disease is the end result of your thoughts and is changeable.
meaning your consciousness controls your body and the way you look...

horus says:

"fear not at all;
fear neither men nor fates.
nor gods. nor anything.
money fear not.
nor laughter of the folk folly.
nor any other power in heaven
or upon the Earth
or under the Earth.
Nu is your refuge
as Hadit your light;
and i am the strength,
force.
vigour.
of your arms.
mercy let be off;
damn them who pity!
kill and torture;
spare not;
be upon them!"
~ Book of the Law

~ aleister crowley

Dragon Princess

i am the representation of the Dark Goddess on planet Earth at this time. but what is the Goddess? she is a triple deity meaning she has three aspects: maiden, mother, Crone. i am in service to the Crone aspect of the Goddess. Goddess is matter, magnetic and resides in the centre of the Earth. she pulls. God is spirit, dynamic and resides in the centre of the Universe. he pushes. you are the child inbetwixt. Goddess and God are electromagnetic energy: two separate forces combined into one force. you cannot have one without the other. they are equal and opposite: a magnetic field creates and electric field, an electric field creates a magnetic field. Goddess, at least what we can know of her, exists in the centre of the Earth as a Dragon.

a real Dragon, not the likes of the cartoons you see on the tube. she is a colossal energy wyrm comprised of the iron filings that make up the heart of our planet. she swims and has swum through the interior of our Earth forever, for it is her body. like how your spirit swims in your blood. you can know the Mother Dragon through the iron in your own blood. the Dragon of God is comprised of light and swims in the Sun. the Dragons of Goddess and God are our heritage and our right as humans to know and to love. some humans come from the Dragon Clan, champions of the Dragons.

  i am a Dragon Princess, for i am representation of the Dragon of Goddess on planet Earth at this time. you want to connect with the Dragon Goddess then offer her your Moon blood or your semen or better yet them combined in ecstasy, left behind outside after your done fucking under the Moon...

whips and jingles

whips and jingles while sleeping? restless sleeping usually indicates a magnesium deficiency. so take some half an hour before bed to get some good zzzzzz's...

venus

"this woman represents venus as she now is in this new aeon; no longer the mere vehicle of her male counterpart, but armed and militant."
~ aleister crowley - *the book of thoth*

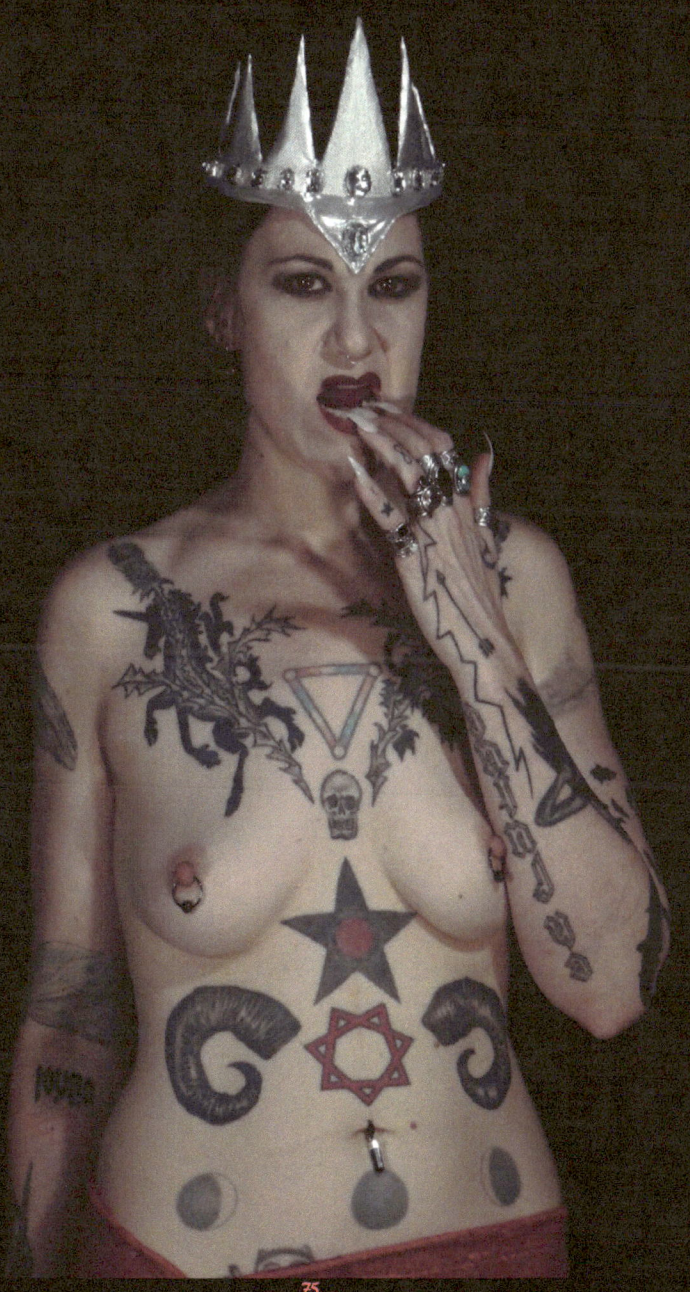

organization

organization of the prime motivator. meaning that the more organized you are, the smarter you are. everything is organization. music is organized notes. keeping a clean closet. studying and learning is organizing your thoughts in your brain. the better you can organize, the better the flow. it is wise to focus upon organization...

hap-dappery

i had a dream three little funny men with big shoes strapped me into some kind of electrical machine in which i had to jump many times very, very high. it was activated by many tiny puppies at my feet. it measured ones hap-dappery which was the brightness of ones spirit of their consciousness. apparently mine was exceedingly bright...

karma

karma is very real. we know this by the conditions in which people live in today. poverty. sickness. war. we want to pity them but truly they are getting the shitty end of the stick for their actions in a past life...

complete reversal

i find it fascinating how the church bullies, tortures and murders a culture and then as time passes that very culture will convert and then zealously guard and defend their new faith.
achieving a complete reversal in their very core beliefs. ahh, the power of tyranny...

trying

they are trying to distract us from the truth... that is we live in Paradise...

fierce

do it. but do it with fierceness...

patterning

find the patterns in things. like cracks on the floor. it is a secret spiritual language...

cover

the logical explanation doesnt always cover it...

set

set. god of the desert, storms, disorder, violence, and foreigners. the darkside of the tree of life. the tree of death. the tree of the dark mother. the tunnels of set. not paths, but jumping. where chaos reigns...

king of the serpents

 one night i was doing ritual in my temple. i happened to have the curtains open so i could see just outside the door, where a water fountain was gently bubbling. the water, mesmerizing me, turned into the slitted eyes of a serpent. we spoke and danced with our eyes for a turn. turns out this serpent was a god. he came to me. though mere words will never do it justice, i can try to explain. he slithered and undulated through the dimensions. he was incredibly large, i could feel him coming like waves towards me. the reality all around me rippling with his power. he made me orgasm by his mere presence. he was the king of all the serpents. all i can say about our meeting is that it was fun...

death

death brings up a lot of emotions in humans. sometimes this is difficult because society has a hard time dealing with emotions. it tends to repress them. it is not death that is the heavy thing, but the emotions themselves. the inability to look at them, feel them, take responsibility for them. you must deal with your feelings and learn to express them. that is why death seems to be so chaotic...

actually do it

you have actually do it for it to count. knowing about it, talking about it and thinking about it do not mean shit...

heal

you cannot heal another person. you can only heal yourself. helping others is an illusion that is involved with vampyring energy and not doing any real good. healing someone conflicts with their destiny. become as strong of an individual as you can. then lead by example. this is true healing...

fine line

eventually you learn to leave people alone instead of agitating them for your own selfish release. you do not always have to speak your mind. eventually you will be lonely because no one will like you. it can be your self centered bullshit that you are projecting onto others. its a fine line...

love thyself

finding your core of self love enables you to fully manifest all of your desires...

healing

"we are all wounded healers. we are all reluctant to become undefended, to become unveiled, and to show what we have inside, whether it is positive or negative. we hesitate to show pain or the wound that we each carry in our own way. we hide it in shame.
  we think we are the only ones, or that our pain is more despicable than anyone elses. it is just very difficult for us, unless we feel very safe. this is our human condition. it will take time for all of us to come out. and it will take a lot of love. lets all give each other plenty of space, time, and loving affirmation. it is through this wound that that we are learning how to love.
  this internal wound we all carry is our greatest teacher. let us recognize who we truly are inside. we are our beautiful core essence, despite the layers of pain and anger shrouding us. we are each individually unique, and it is great that that is the way it is. let us become wounded healers, helping each other to share the truth of our inner being."
~ barbara ann brennan - *light emerging*

air

  one time, i was at the airport, flying home from a trip. i was exhausted, hadnt slept right for weeks. hungry i decided to ask the next person i saw which way for food. it was a little brown man who said he would walk me there.
half way there he said he was a psychic and he wanted to do a reading for me. he said he had an hour for me. i said sure forgetting he had a uniform on. he said he was from jerusalem.
  anyway, half way through the reading, which i totally have forgotten, he asked me to look. i saw the body of jesus and this guy with gold in hands and a gleam in his eye.

then i started to lie about what i was seeing because i then recalled he had what i now know to be a customs uniform on. i remember him saying words like you will move to vancouver, you will break up with your boyfriend. ya whatever. fuck. anyway to divert attention i asked him why he had a tattoo of a guy killing a dragon. then i looked at his name tag: k.george. he looked me in the eye, pointed to his name tag and said he was a slayer of dragons. i just looked at him trying to understand.

i said i thought a dragon was a female priestess. he said no. i said why does customs need you to slay dragons? i said youre a psychic in an airport looking for dragons? i dont remember him answering.

that was the end of our conversation. i really have no idea what it was about other than i know i am now well rested when traveling through airports...

critical mass

it is wise to be free of wasting your time trying to convince unbelievers. leave them to their hell and focus on developing your powers. because in the long run this will assist the world in reaching critical mass, which truly is the goal...

mum

my call is irresistible says the Dragon Queen...

book of wisdom

"in egypt, there was both the egyptian book of the dead and the egyptian book for the living, reflecting all possibilities of what one could experience in life in hieroglyphic or pictographic form. egypt was one of the few cultures that had both a book of the living and a book of the dead. the book of the living was called the book of thoth, from which this particular tarot deck comes from (thoth tarot deck);

it was also called the book of wisdom. within the book of wisdom there were thirteen challenges or tests, and twenty-seven gifts, talents and resources that could assist one in transforming what are called the bardo states, or the problematic or challenging states of consciousness. it is through choice that we can transform the bardo states, or what jung would call the shadow aspects of who we are. 'the brighter the sun, the darker the shadow...'"
~ angeles arriens - *the tarot handbook*

believe

just because i believe in love free of conditions, does not mean i have to participate with you...

threee numbers

three numbers in a row. a key to the new aeon. what were you thinking
or saying when you saw it? pay attention. it was important...

ghosts are within

ghosts of your ancestors are within you. they may make demands. nana. tea. war. luxury. do it!
you can become blissful if you follow the desires of the ghosts within...

duh

95% of the tribal populations were murdered in four centuries by the missionaries of the roman catholic church. millions of witches, gays and heretics were burned at the stake. all the victims gold, land, family treasures were stolen. the roman catholic church is now one of the richest corporations of the world because of this. after murdering all the practitioners of magick, most people do not believe in magick anymore... (?)

playing

playing with ravens this weekend...

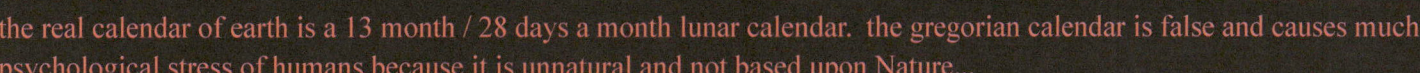

calendar

the real calendar of earth is a 13 month / 28 days a month lunar calendar. the gregorian calendar is false and causes much psychological stress of humans because it is unnatural and not based upon Nature...

belief

believing is seeing, not seeing is believing

silicon is unhealthy

the Otherwise side uses silicon as a net in an effort to capture the bliss juice produced by the human and their feelings... you have been given the task of representing your whole entire bloodline in this fantastic party called the apocalypse...

medicine

medicine fucks with your flow. dis-ease is a indicator that you are living with unhealthy patterns.
it is a signal to change your habits. medicine covers up the problem but does not deal with it

pod people

pod people. people who are so sealed up tight with their beliefs that they cannot see, hear or feel the truth even when it is really obvious. these beliefs can be in any form. there is no point in trying to teach, talk, share or convince pod people of the true nature of reality. because they are locked in and conflict can be their only language.
dont waste your energy

true will

follow your own true will, beliefs, feelings and intuition

olden

in the olden days you would be killed if you cut down a tree... rightfully so

do not tell

simply do not tell other people what to do. what to say. how to think. or how to be

imagine that

when the apocalypse comes your imagination will come to life...

trust

you are only as trustworthy as your word...

oh my!

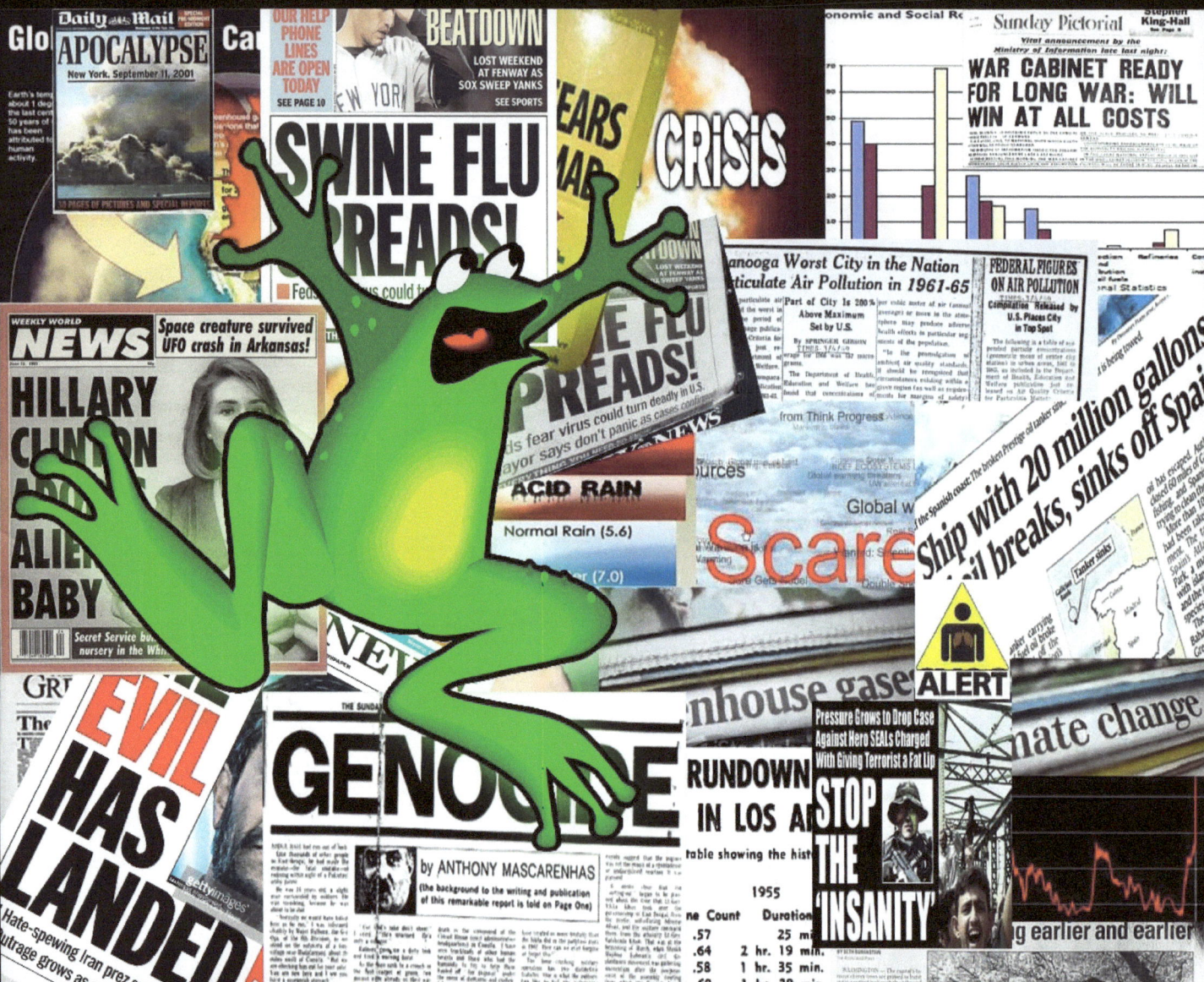

all

we are all one. we are connected by the air we breathe, the water we drink, the space we share and the dna we exchange. our memory and consciousness is stored in the akashic field. our collective unconscious a dark ocean that can be accessed through the akashic field. it is a field that is sub-atomic and vibrates in everything. is has all the memory from the planet since she was born. the memory of every single human, animal, plant and mineral since forever. all of your memories from all of your lifetimes are stored in the akashic records. from the akashic field you can access the skills you have already learned from your past lives. we are all one...

flow

interruptions in energetic flow cause dis-harmony which can eventually turn to dis-ease...

the door

ahh the door!... not everyone knows about it... people have sung about it... once you find it - you can never unfind it... there is only one who can open it (thank Goddess for that)... it has never been opened - but rumour says it might soon... some people think of it as a bridge. hard to say whether it keeps things or keeps things out... but you can certainly hear whats behind it if you listen, but i wouldnt recommend it... there is a key. it causes great strife because everybody wants it. but only the one who can use it - has it. a 'kill you if you touch it' kinda thing... ahh the door!...

you

worship thyself - for the Creatrix is within...

virgin birth

how can they honestly trace the lineage of jesus through joseph to king david if mary had a virgin birth?

1000 years

we are born again and again and again until we learn how to be real people. thousands of lifetimes as a mineral. thousands of lifetimes as a plant. thousands of lifetimes as an animal. thousands of lifetimes as a human. then goal is to become an ascended master. someone who can penetrate the veil of death (the Void) and remember who they are...

worship

worship of a God is called religion. but worship of a Goddess is called a cult. the genesis text always said 'male and female created he them and called their name adam.' adam - adama - adapa meaning human, humankind. it was obviously mistranslated by priests. women were mistranslated out of the bible. even though the original texts speak of the wife of jehovah. in fact yhwh always represented the father, the mother, the son and the daughter. it says clearly in the old testament of 1060 bc. 'the children of israel put away the mother, son and daughter and worship the lord only'..."

axe this

why is the symbol of fascism (am axe in a bundle of wood) on the back of u.s. congress?

cross

the dead guy on the cross did not become the official logo of the holy roman church until 680 AD... (thats almost seven hundred years after the supposed crucifixion...)

enuma elish

the old testament is an exact copy of a text called the enuma elish written in 4000 BC. there were about 30 000 sumerian texts found in sumer. (a city that was in iraq, supposedly the first city of Earth). they speak of the Fallen Angels who came from "heaven" and arrived in their space ships. they also speak of our solar system, but from the other way as if approaching from outer space. pluto is number one, neptune two, uranus three... but pluto wasnt discovered until 1930!? i wonder how a book written 6000 years ago knew more about our solar system than the scientists do now?...

ka template

you have something called a ka template located energetically at the base of your neck. it has three hieroglyphics engraved on it. these are the three lessons you will work with in this lifetime. (~ amorah quan yin - *the pleiadian workbook: awakening your divine ka*.) by being grounded into the Earth is how you record your lessons learned into your blood. then when you get reincarnated again it will be at a higher vibration. your blood holds all of your akashic records. all of the lessons from all of your lifetimes. there is also a magnetic belt around the iron-core crystal of Earth that holds all of the akashic records for all of the humans of Earth...

holidays

if church and state are separate why are all civic holidays on church days? (easter, christmas, st valentines, new years, etc...) the church controls us and most of us do not even realize how much. i mean our whole calendar was created by the church. our holidays use to be in celebration of the Earth not some fucked up alien system. straight lines do not exist in nature. they are a system of control placed upon us. if you are not christian why would you celebrate their holidays?

jfk

the murderer of jfk was proven to be under hypnosis when he did it...

12 zodiac

the 12 zodiac or astrological symbols are named for the 12 members of the monarchy of the Fallen Angels that first landed on Earth 450 00 years ago and started genetically messing with the Guardians of Earth. it is not a system from Earth...

psychiatry? ha ha

psychiatry is bullshit. Fallen Angels made it up in order for humans to feel sick and damaged. they are soulless and heartless. they have no feelings so of course they think emotions are crazy time. real humans live to be a thousands years old or more and there is no such thing as death. death is an illusion. the matrix is exactly the way things are.

Fallen Angels want you to believe that you are crazy... sick... deluded... manic... depressed...ignorant... stupid... wrong... guilty... when really you are psychic... clairvoyant... telepathic... a shapeshifter... a spoon bender... clairaudient... a genius... right...

Faerie Tales are all true. these stories are our ancestral past. our akashic records. our herstory. Fallen Angels are raping the Earth and cast spells on humans to make them sleepy and stupid. alchemical expressions which are singularly designed to make Earth magickians fall asleep.

sleeping spells on magickians just like in the smurfs. they do not call it spelling for no reason. words are spells. so what is advertising then? spells to influence you into buying products or to go to work or war. Fallen Angels feed off of the fear of humans. so they use anything at their disposal to make you afraid.
the more fear the bigger their paycheck. ever noticed how all of our society is based on fear?

everything is war. kill or be killed. take or be taken. win or die trying. everything is based on competition. reality shows, marks in school, government elections. fear of losing. fear is also an umbrella for hatred, jealousy, greed, anger etc. now do not confuse this with righteous anger.

sometimes getting angry is perfect. getting angry and being honest. no! do not touch me! for every action is an equal and opposite reaction. there is a dark side and a light side to everything. once you are aware of the Fallen Angels spells it is easy to avoid them. art and music are sacred spaces where no one is in control...

ok info

thats the tricky thing with controversial information. usually the really knowledgeable person is not trustworthy - for where do they get their information from? the point is to feel every bit of information with your heart in order to feel if it is valid or not.
dont trust the person it is coming from, only trust what information makes you tingle... thats why you shouldnt believe a word i say until you have done your own research! unless i make you tingle that is... lol... it is wise to not trust anyone or anything. not in a sketchy, ugly way, but more in an accepting way...

x-files

the fbi really does have a department labeled the x-files that deal with ufos. the new director of the cia wants to declassify the x-files and let the public in on the relationship between the u.s. government and extraterrestrials...

time for an enema

they found breast milk embedded in the wall of a dissected colon...

sex and death

sex and death are the ways of Mother Nature

grounded

your emotional body is held in your physical body via magnetics. fluctuations within the Earths magnetic field can cause the emotional body to jump out of the physical body. your ability to arrest this process depends on how grounded or energetically and vitally connected you are to the Earth... unfortunately the magnetic fields of Earth have been fluctuating more than ever before and it is becoming progressively more difficult to remain grounded. that is why you will notice more crime, mental illness and general chaos ensuing...

caught with your pants down

   the world is full of lies. lies from the government. lies from the politicians. lies from the corporations. lies from the advertisements. lies from your parents. lies from the religious leaders. lies on the tv. lies because you dye your hair to be something it is not. lies because you get surgery to be someone you are not. lies because you have all this cool stuff but no actual personality. lies to cover up, hide, and run away from the truth. people are told that being fake is better than being real. but the weird thing is the truth glares like the Sun.
   you cannot hide the fact you never went to the moon. you can never really hide your dark roots. you cant hide that there were no weapons of mass destruction. you cant really hide that 911 was an inside job and there was no jumbo plane that crashed into the pentagon. you cant hide your drug abuse for long. you cant hide that your black eye came from your boyfriend. eventually the curtain will fall and the Fallen Angels who are controlling the world will be caught with their pants down and you will be able to actually see the ships in the sky...

pentagram

pentagram = flower = magickian reigning over four elements = elliptical path of venus = the golden ratio = life

focus

you can learn to stop wasting your time being concerned about them
and just focus your time being concerned with yourself.
nobody else matters...
the only thing that matters is finding and following your will
it is wise to allow its voice to be the only voice you really hear...
lead by example.

addiction weakens aura

the human population is easily controlled through addiction...

byblos

the bible was named after one of the great mothers oldest sacred city called byblos
her priestesses kept a great library of papyrus scrolls that the greeks called byblos. (bibles)

morrighan

"mor may derive from an indo-european root connoting terror or monstrousness, cognate with the old english mae-re (which survives in the modern english word "nightmare") and the scandinavian mara and the old east slavic "mara" ("nightmare"); while rígan translates as 'queen.' this can be reconstructed in the proto-celtic language as *moro-rīganī-s. accordingly, morrígan is often translated as "phantom queen." the morrígan is primarily associated with fate, especially with foretelling doom and death in battle. in this role she appears as a crow, flying above the battlefield. the morrígan has thus been likened to the valkyries and norns of norse mythology. she is also associated with sovereignty, and her connection with cattle may also suggest an association with wealth and the land..."
~ wikipedia

love your servitude

"there will be, in the next generation or so, a pharmacological method of making people love their servitude, and producing dictatorship without tears, so to speak, producing a kind of painless concentration camp for entire societies, so that people will in fact have their liberties taken away from them, but will rather enjoy it, because they will be distracted from any desire to rebel by propaganda or brainwashing, or brainwashing enhanced by pharmacological methods and this seems to be the final revolution."
~ aldous huxley 1962

i know you really want to care

1/2 of the Earths forests are gone. 1/3 of what is left is degraded. 1/2 of whats left is
threatened... the corporations keep cutting down the trees for personal
profit of a handful of people... (forests = air to breath) please care about trees...
thats okay we dont really need air to breath...(sarcasm).
go love trees! go celebrate trees! go hug trees! go plant trees! go befriend trees!

rideth

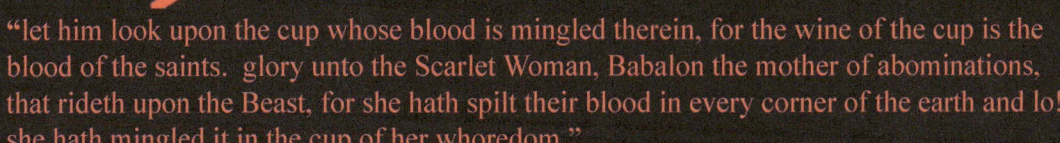

"let him look upon the cup whose blood is mingled therein, for the wine of the cup is the
blood of the saints. glory unto the Scarlet Woman, Babalon the mother of abominations,
that rideth upon the Beast, for she hath spilt their blood in every corner of the earth and lo!
she hath mingled it in the cup of her whoredom."
~aleister crowley - *the cry of the 12th aethyr, which is called loe*

grounding

it is a good idea to be grounded! have plants, animals, crystals in your house.
have a garden. grow your food.
wear natural fibers like hemp, silk, cotton.
buy local and organic. spend time outside in nature instead of around electronic devices...

Beltaine

merry Beltaine. a Sabbat on the Wheel of the Year half way between Spring Equinox and
Summer Solstice. celebrated by dancing over fires and ritual marriage consummated by
fucking strangers in the forest...

aspect

proximity...

terrarium

before the flood there was only a few degree temperature difference on the whole planet,
north to south pole...

fossil fuel

fossil fuel: the dead things on the bottom of the ocean from hundreds of thousands of years
ago that have been fossilized.
so basically we are burning our ancestors for fuel...

when i was held in prison during the inquisition

during the inquisition when they held me in their prison one of the fun things they did to do
to me was hang me upside down by my feet and then tie a 100 pound rock to my hands. it
was a convenient way to dislocate every joint in my body. then i was returned to my cell...
just one day out of thousands...

virgin of eternity

"and the ring of the horizon above her is a company of glorious Archangels with joined hands, that stand and sing: this is the daughter of BABALON the beautiful, that she hath borne unto the father of all. and unto all hath she borne her.

this is the daughter of the king. this is the virgin of eternity. this is she that the holy one hath wrested from the giant time, and the prize of them that have overcome space. this is she that is set upon the throne of understanding. holy, holy, holy is her name, not to be spoken among men. for kor they have called her, and malkuth, and betulah, and persephone.

and the poets have feigned songs about her, and the prophets have spoken vain things, and the young men have dreamed vain dreams; but this is she, that immaculate, the name of whose name may not be spoken. thought cannot pierce the glory that defendeth her, for thought is smitten dead before her presence. memory is blank, and in the most ancient books of magick are neither words to conjure her, nor adorations to praise her. will bends like a reed in the temptests that sweep the borders of her kingdom, and imagination cannot figure so much as one petal of the lilies whereon she standeth in the lake of crystal, in the sea of glass. this is she that hath bedecked her hair with seven stars, the seven breaths of God that move and thrill its excellence. and she hath tired her hair with seven combs, whereupon are written the seven secret names of God that are not known even of the Angels, or of the Archangels, or of the leader of the armies of the lord.

holy, holy, holy art thou, and blessed be thy name for ever, unto whom the aeons are but the pulsings of thy blood."

~ aleister crowley - *the cry of the 9th aethyr, which is called zip*

♦♦♦ the trinity theory ♦♦♦

The Trinity Theory explores the human science of soul. It presents a unique point of view, which demonstrates how you can strengthen your ability to create yourself throughout your lifetime. By showing you how to focus on having a passionate connection to life, it offers you ways to bring balance between both your dark and light qualities. It brings new twists to old concepts by revealing fresh perspectives on ancient ways. It unearths spiritual secrets that have not been available until this jeweled key has unlocked them.

The Trinity Theory is an energetic guide to understanding life on Earth. It is composed of 13 concepts that are distinct, yet harmonic aspects of the cosmology of life. They present genuine guidelines for understanding your place in the Universe. The core principles within flow from the Laws of Nature and represent the inherent formulae of the Creatrix that govern your life. The Theory is simple to understand, yet deep in meaning.

The Trinity Theory is bold. It is unlike any other spiritual system available. With a foundation of the spiral, it is an expression of the instinctive, cursive nature of all living beings. It gives ways to connect with the spiral in your life so you may live in harmony with the world around you, empower your ability to have a strong soul connection and make it easier to find personal freedom. It relates a complete way of life by touching upon many facets of your journey, exploring ways to improve the quality of your experience and revealing how to hold your head so you can see the rainbow.

♦♦♦ trinity sarah craig ♦♦♦

This has been ~ *The Diary of The Scarlet Woman Vol.I*. *The Diary of The Scarlet Woman Vol.II* and *The Diary of The Scarlet Woman Vol.III* are looking forward to your arrival!...

The Trinity Theory Vol. I Human Science of Soul, *The Trinity Theory* Vol. II Energetic Guide to Earth and *The Trinity Theory* Vol. III How to Catch an Angel expand these concepts within and without. They await you...

You can look forward to *The Trinity Theory for Kids*. A 13 volume set of kids books based upon *The Trinity Theory*.

You can look forward to *VITRIOL: The Tale of the Three Gunas*, a trilogy by Trinity Sarah Craig. A memoire of her past-life memories since before time. ♦♦♦

You can connect with Trinity Sarah Craig here:

www.trixxcorp.com
www.facebook.com/thediaryofthescarletwoman
www.facebook.com/trixxcorp
www.facebook.com/theescarletwoman
www.facebook.com/thetrinitytheory
www.facebook.com/thetrinitytheoryforkids
www.facebook.com/vitriolthetaleofthethreegunas
www.twitter.com/trixxcorp ♦♦♦

You can check out Trinity Sarah Craig's Wheel of the Year calendar here:
www.facebook.com/thetrinitywheeloftheyearcalendar

✦✦✦ Bibliography ✦✦✦

Arrien, Angeles, *The Tarot Handbook: Practical Applications of Ancient Visual Symbols* (New York: Putnam Books, 1987).

Baigent, Michael, Richard Leigh, Henry Lincoln, Holy Blood, *Holy Grail: The Secret History of Jesus, the Shocking Legacy of the Grail* (New York: Bantam Dell, 1983).

Biblioteca Pleyades, http://www.bibliotecapleyades.net/

Braden, Gregg, "Awakening to Zero Point: The Collective Initiation," YouTube video, posted by "The Hall Of Records," September 6, 2011, accessed June 4, 2017, https://www.youtube.com/watch?v=JZJa80H62ug

Bradley, Marion Zimmer, *The Mists of Avalon* (New York: Ballantine Publishing Group, 1982).

Brennan, Barbara, *Light Emerging: The Journey of Personal Healing* (New York: Bantam Books, 1993).

Cabot, Laurie, *The Witch in Every Woman* (New York: Delta, 1997).

Crowley, Aleister, *The Book of the Law* (York Beach: Weiser Books, 1970).

Crowley, Aleister, *The Book of Thoth* (York Beach: Weiser Books, 1974).

Crowley, Aleister, *The Vision & the Voice With Commentary and Other Papers: The Collected Diaries of Aleister Crowley, 1909-1914* (Boston: Weiser Books, 1999).

Deane, Ashayana, *Voyagers II: The Secrets of Amenti - Volume II of the Emerald Covenant CDT Plate Translations* (Columbus: Granite Publishing, 2002).

de Vere, Nicholas, *The Dragon Legacy: A Secret History of an Ancient Bloodline* (San Diego: Book Tree, 2004).

Donahue, James, "The Beast and The Scarlet Woman," The Mind of James Donahue, accessed June 4, 2017, http://perdurabo10.tripod.com/themindofjamesdonahue/id358.html

Doreal, M., (Translated by), *The Emerald Tablets of Thoth* (Castle Rock: Alexandrian Library Press, 2006).

Farley, Peter, *Where Were You Before the Tree of Life? (LuLu, 2011)*.

"Forbidden Knowledge," Biblioteca Pleyades, accessed June 4, 2017, http://www.bibliotecapleyades.net/ciencia/time_travel/esp_ciencia_timetravel08c.htm

Gardner, Laurence, *Genesis of the Grail Kings: the Explosive Story of Genetic Cloning and the Ancient Bloodline of Jesus* (London: Bantam Press, 1999).

Grahn, Judy, *Blood, Bread and Roses: How Menstruation Created the World* (Boston: Beacon Press, 1994).

Grant, Kenneth, *Aleister Crowley and the Hidden God* (London: Starfire Publishing, 2013).

Grant, Kenneth, *The Magical Revival* (Lynnwood: Holmes Pub Group Llc, 2015).

Greenfield, Allen H., *Secret Cipher of the UFOnauts* (Atlanta: Illuminet Press, 1994).

Haven, Ross, *The Sin Eater's Last Confessions: Lost Traditions of Celtic Shamanism* (Woodbury: Llewellyn, 2008).

"Hiros," *Heroes*, NBC, 2006, TV episode.

Icke, David, *The Biggest Secret* (Ryde: David Icke Books. 1999).

Magical Egypt, DVD, directed by Chance Gardner & John Anthony West, (Createspace, 2005).

Marciniak, Barbara, *Bringers of the Dawn: Teachings From The Pleiadians* (Rochester: Bear & Company, 1992).

Marciniak, Barbara, *Family of Light: Pleiadian Tales and Lessons in Living* (Rochester: Bear & Company, 1999).

Melchizedek, Drunvalo, *The Ancient Secret of the Flower of Life, Vol. I & Vol.II* (Flagstaff: Light Technology Publishing, 1990).

Morning Sky, Robert, "Terra Papers - Hidden History of Planet Earth," Bibliotecapleyades, http://www.bibliotecapleyades.net/vida_alien/esp_vida_alien_63.htm

Quan Yin, Amorah, *The Pleiadian Workbook: Awakening Your Divine Ka* (Rochester: Inner Traditions, 1996).

Simon, *The Necronomicon* (New York: Avon Books, 1977).

Walker, Barbara G., *The Crone: Woman of Age, Wisdom and Power* (San Francisco: HarperCollins, 1988).

Winter, Dan, Implosion Group's website about Dan Winter - Sacred Geometry & Coherent Emotion, & HeartTuner + BlissTuner, http://www.goldenmean.info

www.ingramcontent.com/pod-product-compliance
Lightning Source LLC
Chambersburg PA
CBHW040053160426
43192CB00002B/57